HOLISTIC SELF-HYPNOSIS

MAKE ELEVEN SECRET INDUCTIONS DO
MORE THAN CURE PHOBIAS AND
ERADICATE FEARS YOU MAY HAVE

A TOTAL TRANSFORMATION TOOLKIT!

BRYAN WESTRA

Indirect Knowledge Limited
MURRAY, KENTUCKY

Bryan Westra/Indirect Knowledge Limited
2317 University Station
Murray, Kentucky / 42071
www.indirectknowledge.com

Book Layout ©2014 indirectknowledge.com

Ordering Information:
Quantity sales. Special discounts are available on quantity purchases by corporations, associations, and others. For details, contact the "Special Sales Department" at the address above.

HOLISTIC SELF-HYPNOSIS/ Bryan Westra. —1st ed.

ISBN-13: 978-1505307061
ISBN-10: 1505307066

CONTENTS

iii

Dedication to Jennifer Bonilla

"You're doubtless well aware that most of the great hypnotic patients wind up referring to themselves in the third person, like little children. They see themselves from outside their own organisms, outside their own sensory systems. In order to get further outside themselves, and help them escape their physical personality, some of them, once in the state of clairvoyance, have the curious custom of rebaptizing themselves. The dream name comes to them, no one knows whence, and by this they INSIST on being called as long as their luminous sleep endures – to the point of refusing to answer to any other name."

— Villiers de L'Isle-Adam, Tomorrow's Eve

INTRODUCTION

Thank you for purchasing this book.

I remember back to a time when I was nine or ten years old and my mother would hypnotize us in the living room of our 100+ year old farmhouse – my sister, brother, and I; that is to say.

We were all relatively the same age with the exception of one year and two days being born apart from one another (Brandon and Brandi were twins). I was the eldest, but it never really seemed to matter considering we were all very close as siblings. My mother made sure we loved each other! Thank you mom! I owe you big for that one.

My mother was a professional hypnotherapist. She had studied under some great hypnotists of her day (primarily A.M. Krasner, but many others too) and went on to become a successful practitioner and trainer herself.

I remember back in those days sitting for long hours at a time reading books on hypnosis and hypnotherapy in her study. I remember times when she would learn a new induction and practice it on us children. My mother had an exhaustive hypnosis library which I would visit regularly.

So hypnosis is in my DNA you might say. It's what I grew up with, it's what I know (like the back of my hand), and it has helped me self-improve my life in ways immeasurable for my imagination to define.

But, what does *all of this* have to do with this book and you (the reader)? Let me explain...

To date, I have written over forty books; many of them on hypnosis. This, however, is the first book I have written on self-hypnosis. There are some personal reasons why I haven't yet written a book on self-hypnosis, but the primary reason has been most books on self-hypnosis (in my opinion) fail to help the reader help themselves *holistically* improve their life path and help them get closer to their dreams and ambitions.

It has taken me a long time to decide what avenue to take to finally write my self-hypnosis book. I wanted to wrtie a book that would help people *not only* cure a fear or a phobia, but also help them to create within them a better environment in which success was be more guaranteed for them.

You see we are not always in control of our external environment. When we're growing up as children we don't get to choose our parents, choose which homes we live in, decide what school clothes we wear (unless we're lucky). There are a lot of things we don't have control over, and for this reason sometimes people feel victimized. It is an *external world* that creates victims. We buy into the belief: "What you see is what you get," and that's all you get. This is not true.

There is another environment which you have total control over, which is your *internal world*. This is one reason why children who suffer abuse tend to go inward and dissociated themselves from reality and embrace rather some fictional reality. This is the reason why we find ourselves in our heads hoping for a better tomorrow, envisioning an ideal environment in our minds, and praying things will work out for us when our futures seem unsure.

This book you hold in your hands is a book which contains eleven self-hypnosis inductions. I've created and hand-selected these inductions for inclusion in this book, and written about them in such a way you can easily understand them and implement them in your day-to-day life. By doing so, you will align the external reality that you see every day with the internal reality you secretly hope and pray for.

Self-hypnosis is more than just curing fears and phobias it can help you, as it has helped me, and millions of others, to live a better life. There's a lot more I could go on and say about this book in this introduction, but I think you will find such a special book more useful if you read it yourself and apply its lessons to your life.

This is a total transformation system to help you feel better, be better, and be more prosperous and successful. It is a holistic approach to self-hypnosis which I have yet to find anywhere else. I hope you feel the same way about it after you've read it and applied its lessons to your life.

Enjoy the book!

Bryan Westra

CHAPTER 1

WHAT IS SELF-HYPNOSIS?

In this chapter you'll learn how to think about hypnosis differently. By different, I mean you'll learn the inside-scoop hypnotists know, but, which most lay people do not know about hypnosis. This chapter will focus your attention on the essence of hypnosis, and present the state of hypnosis as a reverse balancing act between your critical mind and your subconscious or unconscious mind. I'll associate these metaphoric minds with the left hemisphere of the brain, and the right, respectively. Once you learn about the nature of hypnosis, you'll more appreciate how truly beneficial hypnosis can be. You'll also recognize the usefulness of hypnosis and how it can be applied to most areas of your life. Let's start learning.

When a person visits a hypnotherapist for the purpose of overcoming some type of problem, the hypnotist acts as a guide to induce what is known as a hypnotic trance. A hypnotic trance is not what most people think it is. When we think of a trance most people think of images we see on television where someone's mind has been taken over by someone else and they have become mindless beings susceptible to doing anything the hypnotist tells them to. A mindless being is someone who is controlled by someone else. So often hypnosis gets a bad rap, because people think of it as a therapy where they are at risk to losing control of their own mind or having the control of their mind taken over by the hypnotist. For this reason, a lot of people choose not to go to a hypnotherapist, because they feel uncomfortable, insecure, and even fearful that this person, i.e. a perfect stranger, might do something to them to cause them to lose control and do things that they don't want to do.

Guilt can sometimes be the catalyst that causes people to fear the hypnotist. For example, if you've done something that you're not exactly proud of, or you don't want anyone else to know you did, you might be afraid once you are under hypnosis the hypnotherapist will make you reveal something that is highly secretive and private, you don't want them knowing. The truth of the matter is: this is not going to happen. A hypnotist cannot make you do anything that you don't want to do, or that you wouldn't do under normal circumstances. Hypnosis is something you do; not something the hypnotist does. The hypnotist is solely there to *guide* you into hypnosis. You are the one deciding to go into hypnosis. You can change your mind at any time. You can come out of hypnosis at any time. You are always the one in control. Always!

Self-hypnosis is actually a tool numerous hypnotherapists use to help their clients continue therapy without the need of more hypnosis sessions. Hypnotherapy is actually a brief therapy. I truly would not want to see a hypnotherapy client more than a few times. A psychiatric therapist or someone that practices psychology and who treats more severe mental disorders might be needed for longer stents of time. A hypnotherapist, on the other hand, is usually the person you might want to see if you wanted to relieve a phobia, or stop smoking, or something similar to this. In actuality, hypnosis is a way of aligning your mind with a choice that you've methodically decided to make for yourself. For example, if you smoke, and you consciously decide you want to stop smoking, but there is an aspect of you not exactly on board with this idea of stopping smoking, then you might benefit from visiting a hypnotist in order to get help with aligning that aspect of you with the willful aspect of you. The hypnotherapist would be able to help you overcome the habit in a single 60 minute or 90 minute session. Some skilled hypnotists might be able to relieve you of the habit in a few minutes using what is called a 'rapid' or 'speed' induction.

The difference between self-hypnosis and the hypnosis you would experience if you were to visit a hypnotherapist is that you are doing the hypnotic induction yourself. You are the hypnotist hypnotizing yourself, in this sense. The experience of 'hypnosis' is the same, however. You will focus your attention on something; be it an internal thought or idea, or even an external object. It doesn't matter. All that matters is that you focus intently on something. Then you'll use self-talk and visualization to take yourself mentally

So the question becomes: Is it easier to be hypnotized by a hypnotherapist or to be hypnotized by yourself? The answer the question really hangs on your preference. It's a good thing to have someone there to guide you into hypnosis if you have a difficulty visualizing and self-talking yourself through relaxation and hypnotic induction instructions. Another way to think of hypnosis is to think of it as a deep relaxation. It is an intentional deep relaxation, because you are intentionally visualizing yourself relaxing and becoming more comfortable and relaxed.

In today's busy world people are constantly going through the motions of life. Day in and day out these people find themselves automatically doing things which cause them stress, because they've become comfortable with being uncomfortable. For this reason, hypnosis is many-sided in terms of its benefits; namely, because hypnosis begins with relaxation and comfort, and then transitions to the resolution of a problem that someone might be faced with. For example, if you have just started a new job, and you have been tasked with learning a ton of information very quickly, then you might be able to understand how you could become quite over-whelmed by all of the workload in front of you. This might cause you stress and anxiety. The learning curve alone might be something that is outside your comfort zone. So you might decide to go and visit a hypnotherapist in order to resolve this problem of learning slowly. The hypnotist would create for you a personalized program that would assist you with accelerated learning. This could be adapted specifically to the workload in front of you, and it could be suggested to you while in trance that you will be able to learn this information with inside a certain parameter of time. The hypnotist might employ techniques like better retention, stronger focus, and more attention. The hypnotist could utilize these similar associations with accelerated learning to help you learn information that you wish to learn more rapidly.

Once the therapy session was over, the hypnotherapist might give you as a resource some instructions for doing self-hypnosis has follow-up therapy for helping to increase your celebrated learning. The instructions the hypnotist gives you would be unique to your specific situation. The inductions, which are the self-guided process steps, could be identical to what the hypnotherapist might recommend to other clients. The primary difference would be the suggestions you give yourself while you enter a hypnotic trance.

I think one of the easiest ways of explaining the phenomenon of hypnosis versus not being hypnotized is to think of it in terms of two minds. You have a left brain and you have a right brain. Your left brain is responsible for analytical and critical thinking. It is the part of your mind that assesses information and makes sense of it. The analytical mind is categorical in that it likes to separate information into similar groupings. The associations that the critical mind uses have a tendency of making sense logically. For this reason we are able to differentiate and make distinctions between objects, ideas, and even instructions. The right brain is responsible for creative activities. Creativity and the ability to think outside the box or outside of these analytical groupings, if you will, is what the right brain is really good at. We have these two hemispheres of our brain the left and the right, and they help us to function in different circumstances as is needed. The analytical mind (left brain) functions by chunking information down to make sense of it more clearly. From this vantage point a decision can be made, based on what is understood logically. Logic comes by way of deciphering associated patterns that are recognized and coded in the mind's memory. From past decisions we make judgments and form our persuasions which guide our future decision making. In this way, the logical mind's past decisions can create probabilities that can be measured which will predict outcome possibilities. Too many bad past decisions, will lead to a correction that may limit one's ability to take a particular action.

On the flip side to all of this, you have the right brain, which is the emotional mind, or what I like to refer to as the 'other mind' or 'hypnotic mind'. This is the mind that views everything holistically. It takes into account a broad view of everything, which logically can be difficult to conceive of. The hypnotic mind is not controlled by logic or reason. It is beyond our logical reasoning to understand it from a logical perspective. We can define emotions, and abstract ideas; however, we still are unable to define them logically. Take the emotion love for instance; love has been defined by many definitions, for the purpose of the logical mind needing to make sense of it. Making sense of things is done with the intention of being able to grab hold of things, and measure them. Love, we know, is immeasurable. A true logician may even conclude it does not exist, simply because it does not fit into a box, or possess a finite definition that can be agreed upon by everyone. Incidentally, the abstract term God is another example which back up what I am saying. Some people define this term relative to aspects which are logically observable, while others claim God to be an infinite, omnipotent, omnipresent 'something' that cannot be defined. For this reason, some people will even believe that God does not actually exist. The definition must exist if a word is to have meaning, and a word without meaning is deduced down to nothing. This reduction is ironically the complete opposite of being so broad in scope that it cannot be fully defined. I think you get the point. The point is the hypnotic mind (right brain) is immeasurable and illogical, while the analytical mind (left brain) is so specific in how it defines and makes sense of something that it helps us to critically think and make rational decisions.

Outright, someone may want to doubt or disbelieve something, simply because it is beyond their logical appreciation. Suspending this disbelief or doubt is a necessary imperative for letting you fall under the spell of hypnosis. You're actually releasing your critical mind, so that your hypnotic mind, which is beyond comprehension, can help you, where logically you cannot help yourself. You must have trust or faith in this hypnotic mind in order to find the results you're seeking. The best way for a doubter to do this is to simply suspend judgment, have faith in the process, and, then realize the result or effect you wish to experience. Let me better explain.

The metaphor I like to think of in terms of being hypnotized and not being hypnotized is the degree to which we have lessened our critical/analytical left brain thinking and harnessed our creative right brain functioning. When we lessen our analytical mind and increase our emotional and imaginative mind we enter varying degrees of trance. How a hypnotherapist would have you enter trance would be to suspend your disbelief or your doubt about what hypnosis can do for you and have you instead begin to focus on the creative merits of utilizing your imagination and even playing pretend in order to let go of resistance and let yourself play make-believe for a short while.

Another metaphor would be an artist who has taken care of everyday tasks and demands, like paying bills, cleaning house, doing laundry, and so forth, who eventually sits down to draw. Upon sitting down to draw, the artist enters the creative state. Everything else, as mentioned, becomes less and less important, and the artist's focus intensifies on his or her drawing. In a short period of time the artist has side-stepped his critical analytical mind, and entered the 'zone' which is synonymous for 'hypnosis' or 'trance' and now is letting another aspect of his or her self; that is to say, the hypnotic mind take over and produce the result of the finished drawing. Logically it doesn't make sense as to why the artist drew the drawing exactly as he or she did, and this is because that part of the mind was reduced, while the other part was increased.

We are hypnotized all the time, and we don't even really know it. For example, when you daydream, you may very well be engaged in a conscious activity, but for some unknown reason to you and your conscious mind, you have begun to space out and begin thinking about and imagining an entirely different experience from the one that you are actually physically having consciously. Sometimes we refer to this as our *mind wandering*. When your mind wanders you are essentially daydreaming. Another time that you are hypnotized could be when you are engaged in some type of monotonous activity that does not require you to consciously think too much about actually doing the activity. For example, if you like to run, while you are running, an activity that does not require much thought on your part, you may begin to enter the state where your mind begins to wander and think about other things unrelated to running. There are a lot of different terms we use to define the hypnotic state, which we do not ever call hypnosis or trance. For example, you might say to someone, "I'm in the zone," or "I'm in flow," or "I was lost in space." Any of these types of conditions are essentially saying the same thing, which is you are entering an altered reality from the one that you are actually physically present within. For instance, if you're reading a good novel and you become transported into the narrative then you are entering a state of hypnosis. You become sucked into television programs or movies to the extent you believe that you are actually the character or the protagonist, that is, which is actually having the experience inside that altered reality. Psychology has proven this effect, labeling it: *Narrative Transportation Theory*.

The hypnotherapist is representative of the screenwriter who writes a movie script that causes you to immerse yourself so much into the plot you forget about your own reality that you're currently living. In this way, the screenwriter is *guiding* you, much the same way that the hypnotherapist would *guide* you into trance. Usually a hypnotherapist will utilize techniques which quickly have you relax and then begin imaginatively transcending the environment in which you are actually in; namely, in order for you to enter a false reality where change work can happen without resistance getting in the way of progress. This artificial reality can be arguably real to some people, but more importantly it is the perception of realness that makes it so helpful for the carrying out of hypnosis and psychotherapy. When someone has relinquished their insecurities and doubts about what is possible for them to achieve, then it is possible to help them using hypnosis and hypnotic techniques to suggest change in a way that is believable and that which will lead to a change in behavior.

It was Henry Ford who said, *"Whether you think you can, or you think you can't—you're right."* And this really is what hypnosis boils down to: the ability to get out of the way critically, and go *with the 'flow'*. The objective of self-hypnosis is to focus your attention so intently on something that you begin to consciously get out of the way and allow your hypnotic mind to procure it for you—mysteriously as it does so holistically. You don't have to know how your hypnotic mind works logically, is what I'm arguing. Simply letting it help you achieve the result(s) you want is all that is needed for you to know. This will, I'm sure, be difficult, and eye-brow rising for some people—especially those who must be in control, and those who must have a logical explanation for everything. My advice is to get over these limitations, because the hypnotic mind is limitless, and will help you beyond what you logically think is possible. Have faith—I urge you! You won't be disappointed—*I promise!*

CONCLUSION

To recap this chapter I want you to think of hypnosis as something anyone can take benefit from. I also want you to understand hypnosis has two primary benefits: to help you relax and unwind from daily stressors, and to assist you with some type of personal change you want to see achieved. I also want to know hypnosis as something you are completely in control of. Whether you are visiting a hypnotherapist or giving yourself self-hypnosis instructions, you will not lose control of your own mind and nobody is going to take over your mind and cause you to do things you don't want to do or which would be against your value system. It's a good thing to think of the difference between hypnosis and self-hypnosis as being one that is a guided induction process done through the help of a certified hypnotherapist, and the other is a tool you take home to use to accomplish exactly what the hypnotherapist has done. The only difference is you are guiding yourself with your own self talk. For some people it will be easier to visit a hypnotherapist to get the change work done which they wish to have accomplished, then it will be for them to self-hypnotize themselves. Some people would prefer someone's help, while some people will prefer to hypnotize themselves, and be able to use self-hypnosis to help them in many other areas of their life, besides what is immediately pressing.

The last thing I want you to remember about self-hypnosis is that it is a decrease in left-sided brain activity and an increase in right-sided brain activity. This means you are getting out of the way consciously by agreeing to let go of resistance and let yourself be hypnotized, while at the same time you are using the faculties of your imagination in order to create an environment inside your mind that is conducive for lasting change to take place and materialize. Everything begins with a thought, and from a thought can turn into a desired outcome. Hypnosis, in my opinion, is more helpful than meditation on a practical level. Meditation is essentially clearing your mind of all thoughts, while hypnosis is focusing on one idea or thought very intentionally. I hope you have a better idea of what self-hypnosis is now, and an idea of how you may wish to use self-hypnosis to improve your life in some capacity. Hypnosis can help a person alleviate their phobias, overcome fears, strengthen their focus, learn faster, control pain in their body, and an endless list of other possibilities. In truth, you are only limited by your incapacity to think up new ways self-hypnosis might help out your life.

In the next chapter we're going to look at what you need to know up front before you start self-hypnotizing yourself. I want you to think of this next chapter as comparable to the ingredients list for a recipe you wish to cook. Before you can actually cook the recipe it is a good idea to know what ingredients you will need to prepare the meal. It could be you don't have all the ingredients and you'll have to go to the store in order to buy what you will need in order to prepare the dish precisely. This next chapter is going to assist you with having the perfect place to practice self-hypnosis, the right mindset to begin the hypnotic induction process, and some general advice you should know before you start attempting to hypnotize yourself.

CHAPTER 2

WHAT YOU NEED TO KNOW UPFRONT BEFORE YOU BEGIN SELF-HYPNOTIZING YOURSELF?

INTRODUCTION

In the previous chapter we talked about self-hypnosis and I presented you with several metaphors for better understanding 'cognitively' what self-hypnosis is and how it can best serve you. You learned that self-hypnosis can be applied to nearly any problem you may have which would require some improvement in order to get you to the next step in terms of where you wanted to go.

You also learned that hypnosis happens when your left brain activity decreases and your right brain activity increases. I told you that left brain activity represents logical activity. I told you that right brain activity represents more creative, emotional, and abstract activities. Your left brain is responsible for chunking down information into smaller pieces that can be analyzed more intensely. For example, instead of saying you want to make a lot more money, you might zero in on a specific strategy that has been given a name, which would help you to increase your income. Of course the sky is the limits in terms of what this strategy might actually be.

When we think of any overall concept we think more abstractly. When we're thinking of a specific strategy we're thinking more linearly and thus more specifically. Your left brain is structured in such a way that it picks up on patterns that have been formed as a result of these specific groupings or specific experiences you may have had in the past. Because the left brain operates from this vantage point of specificity and pattern recall it is the left brain that often times will reject or doubt something new that is presented to it; explicitly, which doesn't coincide with previous patterns that have been formed and imprinted in your memory bank. On the other hand, you also learned that your right brain is responsible for more abstract ideas and your emotional makeup. Emotions can be understood in terms of logic, but the experience of an emotion at any given moment may be something that cannot always be well-defined in terms of language. For this reason your emotional makeup, which is one aspect of your holistic makeup, has a different role to play in terms of how you process information. You're right brain processes information through emotion as well as covert, indirect, methods that differ from the way that your left brain processes information overtly, directly, and logically. Some people like to refer to the right brain as the subconscious or the unconscious mind. Personally, I like to refer to the subconscious or unconscious mind metaphor as the 'hypnotic mind'. The hypnotic mind thinks in terms of more broader and abstract perspective, whereas your left brain focuses more on specific and reduced perspective.

There are benefits to both your left brain and your right brain processing. Sometimes it is valuable to us to perceive something in terms of its smallest part. In NLP this is called 'chunking down'. If you're learning something new that is highly complex by breaking it down into something specific and then going on to the next item until which time you've covered everything that comprises this total mechanism you can logically learn information much easier in a way that is more coherent. On the other hand sometimes it is important to learn information indirectly to the extent that you will know it without having to focus on it too much. An example of this is how you learned language as a small child. When you learned to speak it was through unconscious processing of hearing other people speaking around you in your immediate environment. When you learned this information you did it easily and rapidly without having to actually think about it and process it logically or analytically. You hypnotically learnt this information without knowing consciously you were learning anything. You didn't have to consciously make the effort to learn the language, you just learned it. In this type of scenario you were learning utilizing your right brain processing. It is also fair to say that you're right brain or hypnotic mind is essential in noticing micro-expressions people have as well as body language that may be incongruent with what a person is logically telling you they want. For this reason, we are able to use both our left brain and our right brain in unison in order to make meaning of what someone is telling us that supersedes what they say with words along. In fact, most language is communicated through non-verbal communication and only a small fraction is communicated verbally. Some people refer to this as using your intuitive mind in order to make better sense of a particular situation or experience.

You also learned hypnosis is something you experience every day whether you're aware of it or not. You learned that hypnosis occurs when you daydream, and you mentally leave the environment in which you are physically present. When you start to think about things outside of what you're involved in doing at the time you're daydreaming, you are entering into what is called a daydream, ultradian rhythm, or hypnotic trance. Regardless of how you define hypnosis in terms of terms, understanding what hypnosis is will be essential when you begin self-hypnotizing yourself intentionally. You'll be doing this soon.

This idea of intentionally hypnotizing yourself or what in this book has been termed 'self-hypnosis' is different than when you begin daydreaming random mental experiences. A daydream can take a random or seemingly random unconscious structure in which you visualize or imagine or even pretend that something has taken place in your mind that may or may not have actually occurred. It's also important to note that when you experience something which emotionally troubles you, such as a breakup or the death of a loved one, this emotional state that you find yourself in is also hypnosis. In this regard hypnosis is occurring and you are unable to logically focus on your work, your day-to-day affairs, your dealings with other people, and so forth. The reason for this is because you are in a mental and emotional state of mind that has taken over your cognition. I need you to fully understand all of this before you go on to what I'm about to teach you next. It's important that you understand what hypnosis is and what it is not.

In this chapter, I'm going to present you with some information you need to know up front about self-hypnosis in order for you to be able to self-hypnotize and have the most success with self-hypnosis. I'm going to explain to you why it is important to put this information to work in your mind mentally, as well explain to you what precisely it is you should know up front before you begin self-hypnotizing yourself. And, then I'm going to present to you how you can take this information and apply it beforehand so that your self-hypnosis experience is greater than before and will be more beneficial for you overall. Then, I'm going to talk about how else this information could be used in other contexts so you can begin thinking about other ways you might apply it in your life, beneficially in terms of, *"What if I do ___?"* (Fill in the blank). At the conclusion of this chapter I will then recap for you everything in a brief summary so you can quickly reference it just before you start doing any of the inductions that I will be providing to you later on throughout this book.

WHY IT IS IMPORTANT TO UNDERSTAND WHAT IS NEEDED BEFORE YOU CAN SELF-HYPNOTIZE YOURSELF IN THE BEST WAY POSSIBLE?

One of the attributes of having information that is going to help you hypnotize yourself better beforehand is the *understanding of what is necessary* in order to most effectively create the types of changes in your life you wish to create for yourself. Knowing this, satisfies the logical part of your mind so that you can hypnotize yourself without any trepidation that it won't work. Another benefit to knowing this information upfront before doing any of the inductions you'll be learning soon is simply appreciating that the experience will be a positive one that affects you in a way that is beyond anything you might consciously anticipate. When you learn this information I'll be teaching you in this chapter, you will be more congruent as well as meeting the requirements within yourself as you move forward with hypnotizing yourself. This goes back to making sure that all the fractional parts of yourself are in alignment with hypnosis and the changes you consciously wish to make in your life to help your personal development as well as your professional development.

WHAT DO YOU NEED TO UNDERSTAND REGARDING KNOWING INFORMATION UPFRONT BEFORE YOU START HYPNOTIZING YOURSELF?

One of the first things you really need to absorb before you begin hypnotizing yourself is what hypnosis is and what it is not. We've covered this in the previous chapter and in the early part of the introduction here in this second chapter. The second thing you really need to understand about knowing information upfront is the type of environment that you're going to be in when you start hypnotizing yourself. The environment is crucial. You never want to be hypnotized when you are operating equipment or when you need to be focused on a particular task—for example, cooking. I can't tell you how many times I have been hypnotized and my mind wandering burnt my meal. I'm going to tell you a brief story.

Once I was cooking grilled cheese sandwiches on a Panini press and being so hypnotized and off somewhere else mentally it wasn't until I saw smoke billowing from the Panini maker that I snapped out of hypnosis and began scraping burnt bread from off the Panini maker. Needless to say dinner was ruined. Of course, perhaps, I was fortunate in that the house did not burn down, or some other tragedies happen. You need to understand that when concentration is needed it is probably is best that you're not hypnotized and able to focus logically on what's in front of you which will require your utmost focus and attentiveness. This brings me to another point.

Hypnosis begins with the narrowing of focus on either an external object, i.e. a physical thing, or an internal memory, thought, or object. It has been said in much of the hypnosis literature out there that an internal thought of something will have a faster response rate in terms of a person becoming hypnotized, versus focusing on an external object. When you focus internally you are closing your eyes and visualizing something, which withdraws you from your external reality altogether, which allows you to become hypnotized more rapidly. You may want to keep this in mind before you begin any of the inductions I'm going to be sharing with you eventually, because knowing this up front will assist you in which method you may want to adopt and experiment with first when you begin to implement self-hypnosis in your life.

Something else you will want to keep in mind before you start hypnotizing yourself is: What is it you're wanting to change in your life and why? Sometimes we reason a change is needed; however, this is not always the case, and even so the changes we think we need may actually not be the changes we really need in order to achieve what it is we want to achieve. For this reason, it is important to come to some consensus in terms of what it is you really want, and why exactly it is important for you to achieve this. This is going to ensure you are motivated, which will help the process in terms of transitioning from where you're at now, to where you want to be in the future. When you begin self-hypnotizing yourself you'll be more congruent when you know why you want to change to happen and specifically what the changes you want to have happen. Sometimes people self-hypnotize themselves and they have a vague idea about what they want to achieve, but they are unable to state it in a way that logically makes sense, and for this reason when they begin utilizing self-hypnosis they sometimes find themselves perplexed by what results they actually achieve. So that you don't discount your own self-hypnosis I want to encourage you to first make sure you understand what problem lies in front of you, what the solution will be in order to rectify this problem, and why rectifying the problem is important to you personally. Once you know this, it is going to be much easier to come on board with this idea of self-hypnotizing yourself in order to start seeing the changes unfold before you after your self-hypnosis session has completed.

The last thing you should really need to know before you begin self-hypnotizing yourself is what exactly a suggestion is. A suggestion or what is commonly referred to as a *hypnotic suggestion* or an *embedded command* or for that matter a *posthypnotic suggestion*, which in layman's terms can be thought of as a mere instruction that is to be acted upon at some point in the future whether through overt means or covert means of communicating this information with you. There are indirect suggestions which are very subtle and then there are more direct suggestions which are very specific and focused. When you're hypnotizing yourself there is nobody to deliver to you a covert or indirect instruction so these forms of hypnosis are disregarded in self-hypnosis. Instead, with self-hypnosis, you're going to be using direct suggestions which you will be giving to yourself in terms of visualization exercises and self-talk internally or inaudibly. When you give these suggestions over to your hypnotic mind what happens is this mind begins to bring about the results you seek. When this happens, the fixed suggestion sticks and before you have time to even realize it, you're acting in the way you wish, and experiencing what you sought.

HOW TO IMPLEMENT WHAT YOU'VE LEARNT IN THIS CHAPTER IN ORDER TO IMPROVE YOUR SELF-HYPNOSIS EXPERIENCE?

By and by, you should have a fair understanding now about what hypnosis is and isn't. You should also have a fair understanding of the importance of the environment you'll be hypnotizing yourself in. You should know too well the importance of being in a nice quiet and relaxing environment where you won't be disturbed for a period of time. All of this is more important than you know. What's even more important, however is distinguishing the overall process for taking all that you've learnt thus far and actualizing it in the form of a mental map, which will bring more conscious clarity to all this stuff. Let me explain.

To begin with you are going to be raising some questions inside you about what you want to self-improve on. For some of you reading this book it may be stopping smoking. You realize smoking causes lung cancer, and a whole host of other health problems. You have now gotten to a point in your life where you want to quit. So for you all in this group, self-hypnosis is being used as a tool to help you stop smoking once and for all. For others, other issues will be the catalyst for adopting self-hypnosis as a tool for affecting changes in your life.

Next, you need an environment conducive for hypnosis. This will be a place like a private bedroom where you will not be disturbed. Try and reduce all traffic noises and other distractions as well, if necessary. The environment should be quiet and relaxing and a place you feel safe and in control. Never practice hypnosis when you are operating machinery or driving. This can be detrimental to your well-being, if you do.

Now, the process will be:

1. Step one: closing your eyes and focusing your attention narrowly.

2. Step two: relaxing your entire body.

3. Transitioning to the induction. An induction is a step-by-step visualization exercise that is specially designed to help you transition from left-brain thinking over to right-brain thinking. You'll start to drop into a mild trance where you become a bit spaced out. You'll go from a beta state (normal awake state) to an alpha state (mild trance state with slowed response times). The alpha state is the day-dream state, or the ultradian rhythm state. An ultradian rhythm is a naturally occurring trance state you enter in throughout your waking day every 90 – 120 minutes. It lasts about 20 minutes. The same conditioned is intentionally being created using a hypnotic induction script.

4. Once in the hypnotic state, you'll then implant suggestions into your hypnotic mind. This involves internalizing your desires using self-talk and visualization techniques. You're essentially, at this stage, future pacing what you want in the future. This means seeing the end result of what you want before you actually receive it. Your hypnotic mind takes these internal imaginings and makes them real, as it's unable to distinguish what is real and what is imagined. To the hypnotic mind it is all one and the same.

5. Finally, you'll come out of hypnosis utilizing an awakening technique. The experience of coming

out of hypnosis is much like coming out of day dream and refocusing back on the task you were previously working on. You simply ignore it and go about your day not giving a second thought to it. The results happen and you have successfully let self-hypnosis work for you in your life to bring about what it was you desired.

HOW ELSE CAN SELF-HYPNOSIS BE APPLIED TO HELP YOU?

I have mentioned only a few contexts like stopping smoking or helping you with personal development initiatives. Self-hypnosis can be applied to many varied contexts—for example, you can help your body heal from a cold faster, relieve pain you have been experiencing, help you concentrate better, help you learn faster, and so many other contexts. You need only to think and ask yourself, "What if I ___" and fill in the blank with whatever idea comes to you. This way of strategizing can be more beneficial than you'll ever know. When you imagine yourself coming up with new ways to utilize self-hypnosis, you quickly discover more ways that you haven't discovered yet. People become fascinated to learn of all the different ways self-hypnosis can positively impact their lives.

Here's a story. I once had a young client who was a martial artist. He practiced Karate. He was really good and participated in national competitions. When he contacted my clinic he was having problems with winning tournament fights. He had a block that was hindering his performance ability. He had created what some would call a jinx that was viewed by him as bad luck.

It only took one therapy session with me, with him undergoing hypnosis, for him to start winning competitions again. He was a great client. He ended up referring me many other martial arts clients. I helped many of these martial artists up their game utilizing hypnosis as a tool for self-improvement. The results spoke for themselves. This is why I almost scoff when someone tells me they don't believe in hypnosis. Usually what the problem is they don't understand what hypnosis is. This is why I've taken so much time on the front end of this book to explain to you in a really great way what it is and isn't and what the process is for 'doing' self-hypnosis.

CONCLUSION

In this chapter we first looked at some specifics things you needed to know. My intention was to make sense of this on the front end by clarifying specifically what you needed to be aware of when it comes to self-hypnotizing yourself. Knowing what to expect on the front-end gives you a roadmap to follow so you know you're on the right path to hypnotizing yourself. Once again I went from specifics and transitioned over to the big picture, where I presented you with how to go about self-hypnotizing yourself in the general sense. I did this to give you the big picture perspective so you could feel more at ease and less confused.

In the next chapter we'll look at the first hypnotic induction and learn why it is effective, what you should know about it, I'll give you the exact steps for ensuring you successfully use it, and talk about using it might be adapted for your specific needs and circumstances. It is important to realize that none of the inductions I'll be giving you have to be done 'exactly' to protocol. You have the freedom to adapt the inductions to fit your preferences. The key objective is simply keeping in mind the process steps I presented you with in this chapter. So long as you focus your thoughts on something, let yourself fall into a relaxed hypnotic trance, give yourself instructions using self-talk and visualization techniques, and come back to consciousness alert and feeling secure in knowing the instructions took and were imprinted into your hypnotic mind, you'll be fine. Let's move on.

CHAPTER 3

THE CONFUSION HYPNOSIS INDUCTION

INTRODUCTION

In the previous chapter we mentioned some specifics that you should know up front before you start hypnotizing yourself. Then, we transitioned over to this big picture perspective of what the processes for self-hypnotizing yourself. The reason we took this approach was to make clear some of the specific things that you should know up front about hypnosis and then give you sort of a map so that you could sink everything together so that everything gets integrated in your mind before you begin this process of utilizing the different inductions that I'm going to be feeding you throughout this book, so that you would have the upfront understanding of how implementing these inductions is going to work.

In this chapter we begin getting into the different inductions that I'm going to be sharing with you throughout this book. Specifically in this chapter we are going to cover one specific induction which is the confusion induction. I'm going to talk to about why this induction is so effective, what you need to know about it upfront, how to actually use this induction to hypnotize yourself, and then think a little outside the box to question what if we apply what we've learned about this induction in other areas of our life and see what happens with that.

WHY IS THE CONFUSION INDUCTION A GREAT ONE FOR GETTING STARTED WHEN HYPNOTIZING YOURSELF?

If you were to study conversational hypnosis and how it is applied to sales contexts and negotiations, you would see straightaway that much of implementing this type of indirect hypnosis is done through the use of confusion. An individual can only process 7+ or -2 bits of information at any given time. So between five and nine bits of information is the maximum amount of data that a single individual can process and still maintain a focus on this information. When you feed someone too much information they become confused. When someone becomes confused they start to blank out and naturally enter a hypnotic trance.

I would like for you to imagine a time in your life, hopefully a recent occasion you can recall, in which you are bombarded with so many things coming at you, at one time, that you literally got frustrated and threw in the towel. There are times in our lives when we need a break from everything going on in our life. Sometimes life gets a little too much for us, and when this happens we start to give up mentally with the course that we happen to be on. I see this happen a lot of times with college students. Many times college students will take on more classes than what they can actually handle. When this happens they start to quickly realize that it's only going to be a matter of time before something has to give, and they will either have to drop a class or two, or else sacrifice the grades they want. So a lot of decision-making goes into maintaining clarity in our lives. If you can remain clear about the things going on in front of you, then you have the ability to focus on what's important, and then pursue it in a way that is worthwhile.

That is important for you to really understand this concept of confusion, and how it applies to hypnosis, specifically self-hypnosis, has to do with your ability to naturally going to trance when your mind becomes overloaded with information. What actually happens is your conscious mind becomes overloaded to the extent that it just seems to want to get out of the way and let your hypnotic mind or unconscious mind passes all the data and information without rejecting anything out right. You really can't reject things when you're overloaded and confused about things to the extent that nothing is really making sense or not or is.

WHAT DO YOU NEED TO UNDERSTAND ABOUT THIS SPECIFIC INDUCTION?

The induction that will be giving you in the next section is the actual confusional hypnosis induction. If you want this specific induction to work for you, then you must allow your mind to focus on the practical task of being able to count backwards from 100 down to the number one. There is more involved, which you learn in the next section, but learning how to count backwards at random can be very confusional for many people. You also need to understand, however, that when you're counting backwards and trying to think about what comes next in terms of which number comes before the one you're on, as her counting backwards, there is a natural tendency for people to want to close their eyes so that they can concentrate better. What you need to understand is that when you close your idea your eyes to concentrate harder you are actually becoming more and more comfortable and tired which makes for perfect environment for hypnosis to happen successfully.

HOW TO HYPNOTIZE YOURSELF USING THE CONFUSIONAL HYPNOSIS INDUCTION?

In this section you'll learn the step-by-step process for doing the actual confusion hypnosis induction. It is good for you to practice these steps so that you get a clearer understanding and greater insight into what exactly is going on with this concept of confusion working to cause people to fall into trance rapidly. I should also tell you that confusion is one of the primary means for hypnotizing people who come to your stage hypnosis event. You'll confuse them and then it will be much easier for you to drop them into trance. Let's learn the sequence, shall we…?

INDUCTION #1: CONFUSIONAL HYPNOSIS

1. Step 1 - Begin by positioning your body in a manner that's most comfortable for you. Some find lying supine on their back to be best while others are more comfortable sitting in their favorite chair. Regardless, create a space free from distractions and full of positive energy.

2. Step 2 - Engage in confusional self-hypnosis by counting down from 100 to 1.

3. Step 3 - Close your eyes when you begin counting, then open your eyes for every-other number.

For example, close your eyes when you say 100, then open your eyes for 99, then close your eyes for 98. This form of confusional self-hypnosis demands enough attention to focus your mind while setting a pattern ideal for hypnosis.

4. Step 4 - Continue until you reach one. Many find it impossible to complete the entire process as the conscious mind becomes exhausted, which opens the subconscious mind for hypnosis work.

HOW ELSE MIGHT YOU UTILIZE THE CONFUSIONAL HYPNOSIS INDUCTION BE USEFUL IN ASSISTING YOU IN OTHER AREAS OF YOUR LIFE?

I mentioned to you earlier that often times when someone is trying to recall information they don't remember quite so well, there is a natural bent for them to close their eyes or squint to permit them to relax enough for the information to surface. The process of closing your eyes, I also explained, makes for a favorable hypnotic trance to easily happen. When you're focused on one thing it's difficult to focus on other things. I also mentioned to you earlier that human beings can only process 7+ or -2 bits of information at any given time. The more intense focus you have on one thing, the less likely it is you will be able to focus on even the five bits of information, perhaps not even four, three, or even to bits of information. And, for this reason, it is important for you to understand that the focus is so useful for creating an atmosphere conducive for hypnosis to naturally happen. You might not have ever thought that focus could lead to being confused about other things, when asked something at random that doesn't relate to what you are focused on. You might also recall a time in your life where you so needed to focus on one thing, but it seemed as though everything else was seeking to rob you of your attention to that one thing.

If we take herein the principle that lies within the confusion hypnosis induction, we begin to understand quickly that redirecting someone's attention onto something else with the sole intention of confusing them, or having them sidestep where their focus should be, can actually cause them to lose sight of the task at hand. When this happens and something triggers a reminder back to where their focus should be, more repeatedly you see a confused expression start to surface on their face, and this confusion will sometimes lead to a state conducive for hypnotizing them conversationally. This can be done simply by continuing to redirect a conversation onto many other unrelated subjects. So in this way this principle of confusion can be useful when you need someone to forget about something, so that you can attain an outcome preferred by you. For example, if someone is focused on sharing with others something about you, and this is something that you don't want them to be sharing with other people, and you know that if you try and voice how you feel to this person, that it will only bring about exactly what you don't want happening. For this reason it's best, perhaps, to confuse them with so much other information that it keeps them from remembering what it is they were trying to tell others about you. In this way you now have learned that confusion can also be a tool for creating hypnotic amnesia, whether in yourself, or inside others, for the purpose of achieving some type of outcome. With the case of self-hypnosis the effect you are seeking is to enter into a trance so change work can be applied so you can quickly achieve success in whatever it is you sought to be thriving in.

CONCLUSION

In this chapter we talked about the confusion hypnosis induction. This is an induction where you are confusing your critical mind (analytical mind responsible for critically thinking things through and accepting or rejecting information) in order that it becomes frustrated and gives up on trying to block information that could be illogical or irrational. This induction is great for bypassing the critical mind and letting your hypnotic suggestions become planted in the field of infinite possibilities which lies dormant in your hypnotic mind. You are able to now imprint suggestions in your hypnotic mind which you want to see multiplying in your life.

In the next chapter we will explore another induction known as the muscle relaxation induction. This induction is great for relaxing yourself and letting yourself enter a state of pure relaxation and meditation. What's more, this induction actually follows suit with a similar exercise many Theraveda Buddhists use as a tool for helping them to clear their minds and meditate more effectively. I know you're going to get a lot of use out of this next induction, so let's hop on over to the next chapter and begin learning more about it.

CHAPTER 4

THE MUSCLE RELAXATION INDUCTION

INTRODUCTION

In the last chapter we talked about the confusion hypnosis induction, and looked at how confusion can be used as a powerful method of hypnotizing someone through forcing their conscious mind to step out of the way so hypnotic suggestions and interesting ideas can be imprinted in the hypnotic mind. You learned that the confusion hypnosis induction is a very simple induction where you're counting backwards from one hundred back to one; alternating between open eyes and closed eyes. When you open your eyes and close your eyes and continue repeating this, then naturally you get to a place mentally where you just want to close your eyes altogether. Actually, this is a physiological response that naturally happens as a result of your eyes becoming tired from so much activity. It is important to note how your eyes naturally blink automatically throughout your waking day as well as when you enter a REM sleep and they twitch. You are not consciously telling your eyes to open and close at will. This is a hypnotic response, which is involuntary. With practice you can intentionally control your eye movements regardless whether or not you blink or not. Some people will blink a lot while others will blink very little. Making a concerted effort to open and close your eyes causes your conscious mind to begin focusing on something it usually doesn't focus on. This creates a natural confusion that consents to let you slip into hypnosis quite easily and smoothly. Beyond this, you also learned confusion can be applied to other contexts in your life. If you have someone that is focused on something you would prefer them not to be focused on then applying an overload technique to confuse them might very well cause them to re-focus on something else instead. This can be especially useful if you have an employer who is upset with you, because you forgot to do something which they had asked you to do. This is a great method of focusing them onto something else, so they reduce their anger toward you. One way to change someone's behavior is to change their state of mind. If you can change their emotional state you can change their reactionary state. Behavior follows thought.

In this chapter we look at a new induction called the muscle relaxation induction. Just like your eye muscles begin to grow tired of blinking, as with the last induction, all the muscles in your body work to help you physically achieve certain outcomes. By intentionally controlling the muscles throughout your body you permit yourself to feel tense or relaxed. This principle of relaxation is important in hypnosis. When a person is relaxed they are more at ease and therefore more likely to do things automatically and without thinking about them. These automatic responses are typically habit-patterns, which have been conditioned or shaped throughout a person's life.

Your physical body is also prone to absorbing certain emotional states. For example, when you feel stressed, often times your muscles become stressed as well. Your muscles begin to tighten and cause you discomfort. There are many theories surrounding why this happens, but in my opinion, it happens because it is our body's way of telling us we are not in sync with our natural state of flow. This term flow can be synonymous with *hypnosis or being in the zone*, if you're a runner, and it can, for lack of a better way of putting it, be thought of as a conditioned state in which everything in your life feels right and you get a sense of inner peace and clarity which takes over your mind and your body. This state of flow is important to maintain. When your body is healthy and your mind is healthy and you are emotionally healthy, then your performance increases and what you are able to accomplish multiplies immeasurably. On the other hand, when your body is feeling tense and stressed, your mind is frantic and not able to think clearly about what it is you want and what changes need to happen in your life, you perform at a much lower level and this can (especially in Type A personalities) create disharmony and imbalance.

In this chapter you're going to learn why the muscle relaxation induction is important for helping you enter the hypnotic state in which you feel in flow and harmony with everything going on in your life. This is a very relaxing induction that reverse engineers relaxation through intentionally tightening the muscles in your body. When your body is allowed to relax, all the muscles in your body align to make this happen. Then, as you become more and more relaxed, you start to discover yourself drifting into trance states automatically and without determination. You're also going to learn what you need to know about this induction to make it work better for you, and then, of course, I'm going to teach you the induction step-by-step. After we've covered all of this you will learn of some practical ways you can use this induction to improve the quality of your life overall.

WHY THE MUSCLE RELAXATION INDUCTION?

Some people tend to store stress in their shoulder muscles and in their back. Sometimes this happens as a result of feeling stressed and having anxiety about your place in the world and what you are able to accomplish were not able to accomplish successfully. There are a lot of reasons why people become stressed, and your physiology and your mental state tend to affect each other. You can feel stress in your mind as a result of your body being positioned in a not so comfortable arrangement. You can also feel stressed physically when you have a lot of things on your mind that are bothering you emotionally. So this back and forth cycle can sometimes mean someone is stressed even when they don't mentally feel stressed. Sometimes we become comfortable with being uncomfortable. Sometimes we build walls around ourselves to block out the truth about our lives, and may say against ideas that could possibly help us. There are many reasons why we do this, but the mass muscle relaxation induction is going to completely relax you. Sometimes you can be relaxed mentally, and sometimes you can be relaxed physically, but more often than not when you are relaxed you're not completely relaxed. The muscle relaxation induction is going to completely relax your mind as well as your body. Once your body and mind are in sync with one another in this relax to state, you will enter trance and then be able to feel a miraculous sense of inner peace emanating throughout your entire being. This feeling is going to benefit you well after you come out of hypnosis. It's going to leave your mind clear and with this sense of clarity you will be able to logically and rationally determine from all the insights are going to be having as a result of this relaxation what is the best course of action for you in order to improve your personal development or your professional development. Whatever it is you're trying to improve upon this induction might be a favorite of yours, simply because it's easy to do and very relaxing.

WHAT DO YOU NEED TO KNOW ABOUT THE MUSCLE RELAXATION INDUCTION BEFORE GETTING STARTED?

Before you actually get into the induction and adopting it as a regular routine in your life it is important to make yourself relaxed and comfortable within an environment that is conducive for hypnosis. We talked about this in the previous chapter along with the importance of making sure you're not engaged in anything which requires your focus and attention consciously. You also need to be ready mentally to apply this specific induction. If you are unable to quiet your mind and find a calm place within you then this induction may be more challenging to adopt at this particular time. In this case you may want to choose a different induction in order to hypnotize yourself. The whole basis of this specific induction is to relax yourself and get your mind and your body aligned so that you can improve yourself however you like, by slipping in hypnotic suggestions while you are under the spell of hypnosis. You also need to understand that a certain amount of time will be required for this induction. It can be for some people a quick induction, while for others it may be a longer induction; it all depends on how much stress you have stored in your body and what all you have on your mind. The less stress you have in your body and the less mental stress you have the easier this induction will be for you and the quicker you'll be able to implement it and see the effects you wish. Lastly, you need to be aware that once this induction is over your body and mind are going to be in a very hypnotically relaxed state that is going to require certain amount of time for you to readjust back into the world. This means making sure that once you come out of hypnosis you allow yourself time to reacquaint and reorient with the world around you.

HOW TO IMPLEMENT THE MUSCLE RELAXATION INDUCTION?

Make yourself comfortable. This induction is easy to implement. You'll simply follow the steps below and commit them to memory to make it so you can easily implement this induction anytime you like. The more you do this induction, the more hypnotized you'll become each time, and the more successful your results will be. Let's begin.

INDUCTION #2 - MUSCLE RELAXATION

1. Step 1 - Position yourself in a comfortable environment. Many find this hypnosis method

works best when lying down with the head supported by a pillow or rolled-up yoga mat.

2. Step 2 - Close your eyes and focus your mind on your feet. Feel every muscle within these weary appendages.

3. Step 3 - Focus on tightening these muscles for five seconds, then releasing all tension.

4. Step 4 - Continue this cycle of tightening and releasing each muscle group until you reach your head. At this point, your entire body and mind should be in a state of pure relaxation and meditation. In this moment begin instructing yourself on areas you wish to work on.

HOW ELSE WILL THE MUSCLE INDUCTION MUSCLE RELAXATION INDUCTION HELP YOU IMPROVE YOUR LIFE?

So you learned what the muscle induction muscle relaxation induction is all about. You learned why it was important and what was needed to be learned before implementing it. You also learned step-by-step how to self-apply it in the comfort and privacy of your own private environment. Now I want to talk to about the benefits of regularly adopting this induction in your life.

In Thailand there is a monastery of their data Buddhist monks who practice a similar exercise to help them to meditate. What they do is tighten the muscles in their body and then breathing a deep relaxing breath out through their mouth let all of their negative energies evaporate into the ether. As they're going through this process their thoughts and anxieties and attachments begin to disappear with this practice. Though I'm not making an appeal for a religious or spiritual school of thought, and nor am I advocating that this technique will alleviate your attentions your attachments to things undesirable, I do know from experience and from many of my students who have implemented this hypnosis induction that the sense of relaxation that happens as a result of applying it, causes a person to become more laid-back and less involved emotionally with outside activities going on in their lives. When you're able to step outside and dissociate yourself from your problems you are often able to come up with strategies and insights for solving those problems much easier. This is because you're becoming more objective and less emotionally attached to the problem. You are also allowing yourself room to hypothetically explore possible reasons both emotionally as well as logically why certain things are happening in your life that are undesirable. Most of the time it is change that is happening around us that we are ignoring in lieu of clinging onto the past. Sometimes we need to let go of the past in order to be mentally engaged fully in the present moment. This starts to take us into mindfulness activities, which can help us to be peaceful even in a world that is seemingly chaotic. When you are able to clearly navigate through life irrespective of what's going on in your life you make better decisions that produce better outcomes for yourself and other people in your environment.

CONCLUSION

In this chapter we discussed a very special induction called the muscle relaxation induction. You learned why utilizing this induction regularly can assist you in staying relaxed and being more objective when it comes to making decisions that affect you and others. You also learned the importance of maintaining equilibrium between your mental state and your physical state. You also leant what was necessary to be understood before implementing the muscle relaxation induction and then you learned specifically what steps to take to successfully hypnotize yourself using this induction method.

In the next chapter were going to elevate to a different level of comfort and hypnosis. We're going to do this using the floating above the world induction. When you didn't think relaxing anymore could happen for you, now comes along the floating above the world induction. This induction is one that has many benefits. You'll feel more relaxed as well is lighter. If you're trying to lose weight than this induction might be one that you would like to use to help you implant certain weight loss suggestions to yourself. When you are able to relax to the extent that you start floating above the world, you know you're really hypnotized, and as such your hypnotic mind becomes open to suggestions that consciously you might not normally believe are possible for you to achieve. You'll learn why this induction works, what you should know before implementing it, how to implement it, and then I'll share with you some interesting ways it can be used to help you in other ways as well. Let's start learning.

CHAPTER 5

FLOATING ABOVE THE WORLD INDUCTION

INTRODUCTION

In the previous chapter we talked about the muscle relaxation induction. You learn the power of tensing your muscles and focusing all of your attention on this tension for full five seconds and then releasing all of the tension including a release of all your mental stress and anxieties, and the things going on in your life which you wish to change. You learn that by repeating the cycle of tightening and releasing you begin entering a state of pure relaxation where you can deliver promising instructions to your hypnotic mind on anything you wish to work on. You also learn the power of meditation and the importance of regularly releasing these mental toxins from your body and your mind. When you let go something, something else has to come in, and that something else is something of your choosing.

In this chapter we talk about a new induction. This new induction is called The Floating Above The World Induction. This is a sitting posture induction where you don't actually have to lie down in your bed or on a couch; rather, you'll be sitting upright with your feet placed on the floor with your palms resting on your precise. What I think is fascinating about this particular hypnotic induction is you begin using your imagination to rise above what you think you are to a more meta-level in order to achieve a state of hypnosis in which you can deliver hypnotic suggestions easily and effortlessly to yourself. If you have difficulty imagining things this induction will help you with that, but it may also hinder your hypnotic progress, and for this reason it would then be recognized mended recommended that you utilize some other induction that required you to less imagine something happening, and instead focus on something until you narrow your focus of attention. Even so, I think this is a good induction for helping you to start to think outside the box and get more in tune with your emotional side as well as your creative side so that you can start thinking from a place of empowerment to allow yourself to achieve more lofty worthwhile goals.

You will learn why this induction is able to help you hypnotically manifest whatever your dreams and desires are for yourself. You are also going to learn what is necessary so you can implement the strategy. I am then going to give you a sequence of instructions that are going to assist you in carrying out this specific hypnotic induction. Finally, you'll learn how to think outside of helping yourself in one dimension in order to help yourself inside of many other contexts.

WHY IS THE FLOATING ABOVE THE WORLD INDUCTION ONE THAT WILL HELP YOU TO DRIVE HOME HYPNOTIC INSTRUCTIONS IN YOUR HYPNOTIC MIND?

The number one attribute of this induction is your ability to imagine yourself above yourself in terms of your consciousness. Now to some of you reading this it may seem as though this type of experience is one that people have with near death experiences where they see their loved ones and stuff as their hovered above their dead body. Let me assure you that it's nothing morbid or anything along these lines, depending on how you want to think of it, rather, this induction helps you to feel lighter and more energized while you undergo the experience of hypnosis. By experiencing hypnosis in this way it creates a different type of environment hypnotically that allows you to become more creative and give yourself suggestions that are more or less doubtful or unbelievable according to how you might think of them consciously. Many people find it beneficial to lose weight utilizing this specific induction. This is one of the reasons I wanted to give you this induction in this book, because I realize a lot of people utilize hypnosis for losing weight and getting their bodies back in shape. Because your lightning your spirit it is symbolic metaphorically and therefore hypnotically that you are shedding weight or dropping the deadweight that no longer serve you any longer. This is one of the inductions I use with clients to help them lose weight and feel great, and I have a 99% success ratio using this specific hypnotic induction with them. I always use self-hypnosis techniques on the backend of my professional hypnotherapy practice. I believe in giving clients the tools they need to help themselves long after our brief therapy is over. It also helps empower the client to believe in themselves and what they are capable of instead of merely relying on the psychotherapist.

WHAT DO YOU NEED TO KNOW BEFORE IMPLEMENTING THIS HYPNOTIC INDUCTION?

So you have something in mind that you want to resolve on either a personal or professional level. It's something that you're using hypnosis to solve the problem of whatever this might be. Because this hypnotic induction does not require you to lie down, it means that it can be used in more convenient and opportune environments. You still need to be careful that other people do not interrupt your hypnosis session, and that you maintain the prescribed safety protocols we talked about before, but what this means is if you're operating out of an office, you'll be able to sit at your office desk and do this hypnotic induction in a relatively short period of time to help you put in the practice and action what you want to achieve. So for example, you are working in an office setting, and you have a 30 minute lunch break or an hour lunch break and you have decided that you want to start losing weight, because you have lived for such a long period of time a very sedentary lifestyle. This sedentary lifestyle has come about because you sit at a desk all day, and do not get the same type of physical activity that a blue-collar worker would receive or someone that is working in outdoors or in a different type of occupation. Chances are you have convinced yourself that you will not be able to lose the weight or that it is something to do with your metabolism or there is some other reason which you won't be able to help in terms of your diet and exercise routine be able to resolve. Whatever be the case this hypnotic induction is sure to help you get back to your ideal weight and help you to start eating better and exercising more.

HOW TO IMPLEMENT THE FLOATING ABOVE THE WORLD INDUCTION?

Now we get to the core of this induction. The following steps are the instructions you'll use to hypnotize yourself. Make sure you're comfortable seated before you begin this induction. Make sure you also will not be disturbed by outside influences that could distract you or cause you to become irritated. It is best to practice this and all inductions in the appropriate place where you will be able to induce hypnosis comfortably. Make sure this is the case. Let's begin.

INDUCTION #3 - FLOATING ABOVE THE WORLD

1. Step 1 - Sit in a comfortable position on the floor or in a chair. Place the soles of your feet firmly on the ground and the palms of your hands on your upper thighs.

2. Step 2 - Close your eyes and begin narrowing your focus on your breathing. Count your breaths and encourage your body to fully relax.

3. Step 3 - Once your body and mind are fully relaxed, imagine your entire being floating off the ground or chair and relaxing in the tranquility of the air. Floating above the earth, your mind is now open to suggestions.

4. Step 4 - Begin working on areas in your life you wish to change. Focus on habits, reactions and physical qualities you know need to be corrected. In this floating state, your subconscious is open to suggestions - maximize its effects through positive intent on change.

HOW ELSE MIGHT YOU APPLY THE INFORMATION IN THIS CHAPTER TO HELP YOU OUTSIDE OF WHAT WE'VE COVERED HERE.

Primarily we have talked about losing weight and using this specific hypnotic induction to help you self-hypnotize yourself around this type of context. The truth of the matter is you don't have to simply use this induction for losing weight. Some people reading this book will find this induction to be their favorite, and something that they can easily do and find themselves hypnotized. If you find that this is true for you then by all means use this hypnotic induction to help you stop smoking, reduce anxiety, fight the common cold, or whatever the case happens to be. If we go to this context of fighting the common cold, which all of us sometimes get, what's nice about this induction is you don't have to be at home sick in bed in order to help your automatic immune system autonomic immune system kicking the high drive to start fighting your illness. In fact Y at home in bed and getting plenty of rest and sleep tells your hypnotic mind that it is important that you rest, and that in time you will start to get over this cold. If this isn't something you can do, however, you'll find it empowering to know that if your at work, on break, sitting at a desk or table trying to eat your lunch and take your medicine, that this specific hypnotic induction will be more convenient for you to close your eyes and start imagining yourself floating above the world so that you can give yourself the right types of instructions to help you fight off that cold and get well soon.

A final point I want to make in this section is the power of suggestion. I remember when I was nine or 10 years old my mother let me read a book that she had purchased called the magic of believing. This book turned me onto a lot of different ideas that I had no recollection of prior to reading the book. I guess what I'm trying to say is it's almost a guarantee that positive verbiage helps people in many more ways than what's understood. When you smile at someone or talk to them in a friendly manner and complement them and share some positive feedback with them he can have a stimulating effect that prompts them to achieve even more. He can also help them improve their relationships by being in a better mood and staying the course in terms of furthering themselves personally and professionally. The power of belief is something so hypnotic in nature, and yet we don't ever think of it as being hypnotic. A simple suggestion that someone gives you is something that you can opt to believe or dismiss and forget. We've all experienced times in our lives when someone has said something to us that rubbed us the wrong way, that when we walked away from that person and when about our day we just simply could not forget. This type of poisonous thought can destroy our happiness, but only because we let it. When you're giving yourself self-hypnosis instructions it's important to realize that there is an emotion that parallels and is congruent with knowing that something positive will come about from the hypnosis session we've just experienced. When you come out of hypnosis I want you to know the difference between knowing that the instructions have taken hold and been imprinted in your hypnotic mind, and the difference between when they have not. Sometimes when you undergo self-hypnosis you may have some doubts and hesitations after a session has happened. I want you to remember that you can always go back and do the session again when the timing is right for you. Sometimes it's our mindset or the state of mind where currently in that has an impact on whether a hypnosis session is successful or not. More often than not your hypnosis sessions will be highly effective and work instantly to start bringing good and positive things into your life. It's good that you understand the differences between how you feel when you know something has taken hold and that positive changes are bound to happen and you have a knowing that your hypnosis session has worked for you in the difference between when it doesn't seem quite so strong or as powerfully impactful as what you think it should. You will start to achieve this the more you do hypnosis, and the more you do hypnosis the more results you will begin to achieve in your life. You will also continue building value in your mind as to what hypnosis can help you achieve.

CONCLUSION

In this chapter we talked about a new hypnotic induction called above the world hypnotic induction. Floating above the world means seeing things from a different vantage point. It means stepping outside of your normal everyday reality in order to objectively discern where changes need to be made versus what you're already doing right. This is huge when it comes to your personal development. Eventually using this hypnotic induction you will begin to see a powerful overhaul start happening starting to happen in your everyday life. You have to think that there are so many different choices and possibilities out there, but as human beings were limited on what we observe at any given moment. Sometimes we all will have bursts of insights that seem ingenious. When this occurs we feel utterly empowered and begin having faith in our abilities to pursue changes more proactively. On the other hand, sometimes life is stagnant, and we don't always get those insights that we really would like to. When this happens and things turn negative for us this can negatively compound other areas of our life which need improving spiraling them substantially out of control.

In the next chapter we will be looking at yet another induction known as the lost in breath induction. This induction is going to help you become more in tune with your body and your breathing. You'll discover a powerful way to correct problematic conditions you may be facing, while asserting positive changes in your life. Your breathing will become a metaphor for exiting toxic energy every time you exhale outwardly. This induction is also going to allow you to speak to yourself like a caring parent speaking to a child. Instead of speaking out loud however, you'll be silently speaking to these areas utilizing self-talk.

CHAPTER 6

THE LOST IN BREATH INDUCTION

INTRODUCTION

In the previous chapter you learned a hypnotic induction that can easily be applied when in an upright sitting posture. This posture may be one that you will want to use when you're in a private office setting, or sitting somewhere anywhere besides your own domain. The interesting thing about this induction is that it lets you step outside your normal 'everyday' reality so that you can experience a shift or change that can be relatively refreshing.

In this chapter you'll learn a new induction called: The Lost In Breath Induction. It is named this for good reason; namely, because it utilizes your breath in a special way that rids your body of negative energy and mental distress, while allowing positive vital energy to permeate your being. This induction can be used for helping you heal yourself physically and mentally. In a clinical setting I have used it to help clients improve immune health, and even overcome common colds. Of course, as is true with all hypnosis and hypnotherapy—always consult the advice of a licensed healthcare provider for mental disorders or health related issues before employing hypnosis as a tool to aid in recovery.

WHY LEARN THE LOST IN BREATH INDUCTION?

For starters this induction is almost meditative in so many words. You'll be relaxing your body, letting your mind suspend belief, helping yourself to accept that changes need to be made in order for you to self-improve, and it is extremely easy and never boring. Used regularly, I think you'll benefit extraordinarily from implementing this hypnotic induction as a regular routine to self-improve aspect of your life which needs work.

I think it is also important to keep an open mind whenever applying self-hypnosis, because so much of your success with it will depend on how receptive you are to it. It's a paradox of sorts. Make sure you fully want to be hypnotized and want to gain the results from self-therapy. Let's learn more about this induction.

WHAT DO YOU NEED TO KNOW UPFRONT ABOUT THE LOST IN BREATH INDUCTION?

To begin with you should realize that this approach begins with you engaging in a physical act. Specifically, you will be touching your belly just above your belly button. For this reason I recommend you be in a nice quiet, private, environment where you can relax and where you won't feel self-conscious about physically doing the induction. Next, you must realize that this induction will begin with you addressing by assessing certain aspects about your life and your habits that may be uncomfortable emotionally dealing with. This happens before you start to let in more positive thoughts. In this way you might think of this technique much like that of a 'boot camp' where you are broken-down so that you can be built back up. Not everybody responds well with addressing parts of themselves that are less than perfect. It is important to keep this in mind before actually doing the induction. So, with all of this out of the way, let's learn the induction.

HOW-TO DO THE LOST IN BREATH INDUCTION?

The lost in breath induction is only four steps. In this way it will be easy for you to remember what you need to in order to implement the induction. Follow the steps below and experience hypnosis in a way that will get rid of the 'bad stuff' and pave the way for the 'good stuff'.

INDUCTION #4 - LOST IN BREATH

1. Step 1 - While sitting or lying down, close your eyes and place your hands on your diaphragm; located a few inches above your belly button.

2. Step 2 - Begin breathing deep breaths, which cause your belly to extend. Make sure your shoulders don't rise with each breath.

3. Step 3 - Listen to the sounds of your body as life-giving oxygen flows in, and toxic energy rushes out with every exhale. Count your breaths. After 30 deep inhales and exhales, begin instructing your mind.

4. Step 4 - Remove yours focus from breathing and isolate areas of your body and mind you wish to tend to. Silently speak to these areas, call them forth for repair. During this state, begin correcting habits and emotions that aren't beneficial for

life. Close the session by returning your focus to your breathing and slowly opening your eyes to rejoin the physical, conscious world.

HOW-ELSE CAN THE LOST IN BREATH INDUCTION BE USED TO HELP YOU SELF-IMPROVE?

There are many people who will tell you (maybe you're one of these people) how important implementing a regular meditation routine in their lives have helped them to feel more peaceful and less anxiety ridden. This induction is a great one to adopt in everyday continued improvements. You can use this induction when you get sick to help you relax and feel less discomfort, but also to help you internalize positive changes and overcome your cold mentally which can aid in assisting with the physical and debilitating aspects of the cold. Keep in mind however that a cold may be a metaphor for something needing to happen in your life. Perhaps, for example, you are stressed out at work, or don't want to face a certain problem you may be facing, and so for this reason a cold may be an unconscious 'answer' (or 'excuse'—depending on how you look at it) to get you out of having to confront the problem or else delay it so you have more time to think over what you want to do. Unfortunately, if this is the case, it would be much nicer if we came up with better solutions than getting sick. Again, this all happens at the unconscious level.

Speaking of this, let me just have you think about something: Before we knew what germs were or how viruses worked, humankind had other ways of thinking about 'cold' and other ways to 'fix' being sick. At least they thought the solutions were helpful, even if they weren't founded in science. When we don't know something consciously (i.e., scientifically) then it becomes a matter of subconscious understanding. I think it is interesting that colds and getting sick used to happen to come about as a result of subconscious interpretation. Today, with scientific explanation, we know more about how colds work from a conscious level of thinking. Just some food for thought, though it doesn't have to necessarily relate to the reasons you may want to utilize this specific induction. Take a moment to think of how else you may be able to profit from this induction. I'm sure, like most people, you'll come up with some useful examples of different contexts where you might apply this induction.

CONCLUSION

In this chapter you learned about the lost in breath induction. You discovered why it can be used to help a person breath out negative energy, while inhaling positive 'life giving' oxygenated energy that is useful for relaxing and improving the self. In many ways you discovered through inference that this induction can be used to help you come face to face with your true self, and provide you with a positive picture of what is possible when you regularly implement this induction into your daily routine. You also learned how to implement this pattern with four easy to remember steps. Probably, and hopefully, you took a few minutes to think about some different contexts in which you can apply this induction, as well.

In the next chapter you'll learn Experience Rewards from Future Goals Induction. This induction is unique in that it is specific to goal setting. In NLP and Hypnosis we have a concept which we define by the term 'future pacing'. Future pacing is envisioning a future result as having already transpired—for example, you might think about how you will feel and what life will be like when you win a lottery. Now, perhaps you've never won a lottery before, and certainly have not won one yet, however you can envision what winning might be like, how you'd spend the money, and the changes you might make to your lifestyle, and what winning will feel like when you come to the realization you've won. For example, you might feel excited, jubilant, and overjoyed. Chances are you won't be disappointed to discover you've won. That just doesn't make sense, does it? Anyway, this is future pacing. This concept is being applied to the induction you'll be learning about in the next chapter. Let's learn more.

CHAPTER 7

THE EXPERIENCE REWARDS FROM FUTURE GOALS INDUCTION

INTRODUCTION

In the previous chapter you learned the lost in breath induction. You learned how to implement it successfully. You learned under what types of scenarios you might want to employ using it. You also learned what you needed to know upfront, before implementing. And, you also learned to think in broader terms what other contexts and ways using that induction might serve you usefully/purposefully.

In the this chapter we turn away from letting go of old beliefs and patterns that no longer resonate with us anymore, and inhaling positive changes to occur in order to let ourselves internalize the necessity for changes and come on board mentally with making such changes. In this chapter we'll look at a powerful way of preparing for changes to happen using a hypnotic technique known as future pacing. Future pacing is seeing an outcome in our mind as already having happened, before it happens. Before something has happened it is merely 'potentiality' or some result that 'could' happen to come about. Seeing the end in mind, is what many success coaches tell their clients in order to get them to step outside of one emotional state and enter into a different emotional state. People make decisions based on emotions they are feeling at a given time. This induction is freeing in the sense that it opens us up to experiencing reality before it happens—mentally. When you can do this you can see the potential effects of your actions before actually acting. This way, you can determine ahead of time if what you think you want is actually what you want in the first place. It's powerful stuff. Let me share more with you.

WHY YOU WANT TO LEARN THE EXPERIENCE REWARDS FROM FUTURE GOALS INDUCTION

Let's think for a moment about the importance of setting goals. You may believe that people who set goals are more likely to achieve in life what they desire to achieve over people who do not set goals for themselves. The thing to really understand is: goal setting is measuring a process in order to determine logically in our minds when we can 'expect' to accomplish something (i.e., a goal) we want to accomplish. When we know the steps involved we can see the big picture and determine if it is actually something worth pursuing or not. It helps us to wrap our minds around what's involved to get us to where we want to be in life. Goal setting is metaphorically the roadmap that we use to guide us toward a destination (i.e., a goal). Without goal setting we're navigating in the dark, hoping to get to where we want to be, yet somewhere deep within our psyche most of us assume we'll not get there unless by some chance miracle. In other words our chances of getting what we want drastically increases when we have a map that represents the journey and gives confirmation to us that we're on the 'right' path whenever we pass another landmark (benchmark). Mentally we use probabilities to create beliefs about what we think an outcome will be. If you believe there is a 90% chance you'll will the lottery then chances are you will be more motivated to buy a lottery ticket, because you believe there is a very likely chance you'll win. On the other hand is you believe there is only a .000001% chance you'll win the lottery, then you'll likely be less motivated to spend a dollar and buy a ticket.

The induction I'm going to teach you in this chapter is going to help you employ some of this thinking in a positive way that will help you focus on your goals, isolate them, and instead of focusing on the 'how' in terms of how to achieve the goal, you'll be focusing on experiencing the potential effect you will receive were you to achieve the goal. This is going to make the goal more alive in your mind, and help you to feel mentally in your mind what the experience will be like after it is achieved. A powerful thing happens when you change from feeling like something is a potential probability to something is a destined outcome. You shift from believing that something is possible, to knowing that something is without doubt going to occur for you. Thinking something will happen and knowing something will happen have two totally different feeling attached to each. When you know something will happen you feel completely confident it will happen. There's security, absolute faith, and utter confidence it will result— attached to a 'knowing'. There's only hope, a deep desire, and still uncertainty (though it may only be minimal probabilistically) that something will happen. Two completely different sets of emotional connections attached, yet the difference is night and day in terms of when and how something actually will come about as reality. We act and make decisions based on emotions. The key with this induction is that it will help you achieve the 'right' emotions to experience to ensure you take the right actions to get you to where you want to be in terms of what goals you set for yourself.

WHAT YOU MUST KNOW TO IMPLEMENT THE EXPERIENCE REWARDS FROM FUTURE GOALS INDUCTION.

Upfront you must realize that this is easier than perhaps mentally you may be making of it up to be in your head. Do not get bogged down by terms like 'future pacing' or the technicalities of statistical inferences. Instead, make yourself receptive to receiving what you want out of life in terms of your personal goals for you. Also realize that you'll be doing some visualizations where you will be imagining something you want to happen as already having happened. Keep in mind also that if you operate more from an auditory sense or a kinesthetic sense that you can imagine what this experience will sound like or what it will feel like having already happened. This can also be combined with visualizing it to instill a more real sense of it having already happened. You must also realize that implementing this induction can really help you build your faith and belief that something once per-haps thought to be impossible is actually believably go-ing to result. This can help you make different decisions, which are more aligned with what you want, as op-posed to what you think you can achieve based on your beliefs alone. Lastly, let me share that this induction is no more challenging than any of the others I've presented you with thus far, nor will present to you in the future. Let's learn it!

HOW TO IMPLEMENT THE EXPERIENCE REWARDS FROM FUTURE GOALS INDUCTION.

Like anything new, take your time the first couple times through. Practice will breed familiarity, which will attribute to you experiencing greater success with this implement. It is a good idea incidentally to take this 'take it easy' approach with all of the inductions throughout this book. I've found that the easier you make things for yourself on the front end, the deeper into hypnosis you will go. Here are the steps to implement this induction.

INDUCTION #5 - EXPERIENCE REWARDS FROM FUTURE GOALS

1. Step 1 - While sitting or standing, close your eyes and focus on the goals you wish to accomplish. Narrow your attention on no more than three   specific   goals.

2. Step 2 - Once these goals are isolated, allow your mind to drift into the future. What are the rewards for these goals? Don't focus on what you must do to accomplish these goals, but rather, narrow your attention on what's to be gained when they're accomplished.

3. Step 3 - Remain secure in the knowledge that you'll accomplish the necessary goals to receive the much-deserved rewards. After several minutes of imagining these rewards, bring yourself back to reality and continue forward with the work required to turn these rewards into reality.

HOW ELSE MIGHT YOU BENEFIT FROM THIS INDUCTION?

There are so many actual techniques clinicians use to help their therapy clients overcome different types of problems they are facing. My advice when applying this to a self-hypnosis psychotherapeutic context is that you first think about the problem you may be faced with. Once you have done this, ask yourself: What self-hypnosis induction you've discovered in this book is going to work best for helping you overcome this specific problem? In many cases, people have found that this specific induction works well when they want to achieve something they might be on the fence about in terms of if they can actually achieve it or not. Typically, when you apply this induction the resulting phenomenon will be that you'll get a sense of "I can do this!" attitude that may be exactly what you need to start taking action in that direction. In so many words, this induction can be very motivational and help inspire inspiration in a person so that they can begin falling in love with their dream all over again. When they do, they discover that their dream is worth pursuing and that it is possible for them to achieve what they wish. This hypnotic induction is mental alchemy that takes thoughts and turns them into reality (form/substance).

CONCLUSION

In this chapter we explored an induction that results in a person experiencing an outcome mentally before actually experiencing it outwardly. We have an inner world of experiences just like we have an outer world of experience. We can be doing something on the outside, like some activity; while at the same time be having a thought about something altogether unrelated on the inside. This living in two world's phenomenon is hypnosis in action. You're experiencing one truth with your conscious mind, living outside yourself; while also experiencing another truth with your hypnotic-mind (subconscious mind), living inside yourself. When we look at life through this prism of duality it can sometimes take us to thoughts that are philosophical in nature—we question reality, we wonder about the meaning of it all, we contemplate abstract truths (hoping to make them less ambiguous through critical thinking), and so forth. The take away with this chapter is that you can harness the power of your hypnotic-mind and create for yourself endless experiences of success that will help you achieve the right 'emotions' or 'feelings' that will help to guide you in the right direction when pursuing whatever path you chart out for yourself.

In the next chapter we will explore a hypnotic induction called: Return to Previous Mindsets. This induction implements using NLP sub-modalities to have you utilize your senses from a past memory, where you felt empowered, stronger, and able to conquer the world on your terms. Essentially you will be contrasting the emotional state you've found yourself in lately, to that earlier empowered state, and by creating allowing them to occupy the same space, you'll let yourself grab back hold of the resourcefulness of the earlier state and bring it back into the future state where you feel less empowered. This induction is a good one should find that you are not your usual self. This technique can help you regain resourcefulness and get back to where you need to be. Often times sports professionals will apply this technique and find themselves making shots again, performing at peak levels, and winning more games. I think you'll find it useful in the right contexts. Let me share it.

CHAPTER 8

THE RETURN TO PREVIOUS MINDSETS INDUCTION

INTRODUCTION

In the previous chapter we looked at an induction to help you set goals by future pacing desired outcome events. You learned how emotions play such a pivotal role in action (i.e., behavior). Sometimes it is a wrong action which results from possessing a wrong emotion. If you look at two different emotions you see two different results likely to happen were someone to experience one over the other. In order to exhibit and possess the right emotion to possess the right state of mind, which will result in you carrying out the right actions, in order to get you the results you want, you learned about future pacing. Future pacing is an amazing induction, because it helps us to step into the reality we want to have shown up in our lives before it actually shows up. So we are starting in the mind first, and then from here we are receiving the right emotional response welling up in us when we envision what experience we want to experience, and once this specific emotional reaction occurs we are then more likely to carry out the right types of actions to get us what we want.

In this chapter we are going to look at a hypnotic induction which is actually the inverse of the previous induction. Maybe you find yourself in a situation where you're not feeling all that resourceful? Perhaps you feel as though you have jinxed yourself and now can't get back up on the horse? Maybe you're afraid of failure and now find yourself in a state that is not resourceful whatsoever. At this stage, chances are whatever actions you might take will not lead you to getting back up on the horse again. For this reason, this next induction is going to help you regain a state of resourcefulness 'mentally' so that it becomes a natural progression for you to move forward with success again. Specifically, we are going to back in time, to a previous encounter that you have had in which you were so empowered and resourceful, that failure just will not be an option for you. Let me explain.

WHY YOU SHOULD LEARN THE RETURN TO PREVIOUS MINDSET HYPNOSIS INDUCTION?

The return to previous mindset self-hypnosis induction is one that is going to allow you to get back to a state of mind in which you felt resourceful and empowered. Notice, how when you are feeling empowered, you do things quite differently in terms of your actions than what you might do when you're feeling less than empowered and fearful. When people are afraid their minds are haunted by this thought that they will not be able to achieve whatever it is they aspire to achieve. This is a thought virus that infects your ability to move forward and continue on being successful. We have all experienced this type of phenomenon at some point or other in our lives. The way we get rid of this virus is to reboot our system back to an earlier operating system. In your memory you have saved experiences, emotions, thoughts and ideas, so that you are able to re-experience or as we like to call it in hypnosis—'revivify' earlier experiences mentally, which can drive you back to the state of being resourceful and feeling empowered.

WHAT DO YOU NEED TO UNDERSTAND FIRST IN ORDER TO IMPLEMENT THE RETURN TO PREVIOUS MINDSET SELF-HYPNOSIS INDUCTION?

The first thing you need to understand about applying this hypnotic induction is a brief understanding of NLP sub modalities. A sub modality is very simply a specific observation about a visualized, auditory, kinesthetic, gustatory, or olfactory experience. The idea here is when you are recalling a previous event in your mind, that you focus specifically on what you can pick-up on with your senses—the color contrasts taking place in your mind, what smells you are smelling at that particular moment, what you are hearing both consciously and unconsciously, how you're feeling at that particular moment in a very specific and conscious perception, and you get the point. So what you want to do is when you're recalling a former memory is to consciously go back in and look at all the things going on around you and pay particular attention to those things you may never have been consciously aware of at the time you were actually experiencing the event originally. What the sub modalities do is allow us to be able to re-create in our minds a more dynamic and realistic recollection of a former event. When this happens we gain clarity in terms of our emotional well-being at that particular time. This is important, because when you're applying this hypnosis induction on yourself you need to be able to really experience the sensations you felt back then, so you can carefully contrast those with the sensations you're feeling right now. And you'll understand more clearly what I'm talking about in the next section when I walk you through the process of how to do this specific induction.

HOW TO IMPLEMENT THE RETURN TO PREVIOUS MINDSET SELF-HYPNOSIS INDUCTION?

Now I want to walk you through step-by-step what you need to understand and follow to successfully implement this self-hypnosis induction. In many ways this induction is a lot of fun to put into action, because the very act of contrasting one thing to another can be very liberating and insightful. When you contrast two objects similar in nature; looking for discrepancies and how they are different from one another, you start to see things differently than you before perceive them to be. An object that looks like another object in a general sense, can, when closely analyzed, be perceived to be quite different from each other in more detail sense. By closely analyzing something and comparing it to another object you get to utilize your conscious mind and apply your critical thinking skills in order to see anomalies and other variances you may not have really understood prior to this. So let's get to the learning.

INDUCTION #6 - RETURN TO PREVIOUS MINDSETS

1. Step 1: Think of a time in the past where your motivation, confidence and optimism were at their   peak.

2. Step 2: Imagine you're back in that physical setting where these positive emotions were their strongest. Feel the world around you as it felt then. Hear the sounds and smell the aromas that filled your conscious world during this time.

3. Step 3 - Allow your mind to fully re-live these moments. Focus on the inward feelings you had. The feeling of pure confidence and success.

4. Step 4 - Combine these past feelings with a current situation. Allow these two worlds to exist in the same space. Direct your mind to adopt these emotions once again. Imagine your current world be shaped and altered by these high-performing emotions.

HOW ELSE MIGHT THEN RETURN TO PREVIOUS MINDSET SELF-HYPNOSIS INDUCTION SERVE YOU IN TERMS OF OTHER CONTEXTS?

Sometimes we discover that were not always functioning at our peak level. This doesn't necessarily have to be regarding a particular problem area that you are currently experiencing, it can also be very simply changes in your mood throughout the day. When you take notice of how you feel in the conscious sense, you start to see at certain hours of the day you tend to focus better than during other hours of the day. Much of this has to do with ultradian rhythms. Ultradian rhythms are cycles of hypnotic trance states we fall into each and every day in which we are unaware we are under the spell of hypnosis. Normally, you are consciously alert and focused more so than not on a given activity for approximately every 90 minute period of time you are awake. Just like the seasons change and we experience changes in waking activity; that is to say, winter is a slowing down period, while spring and summer tend to be more active periods of time for most people—the same can be said of these ultradian rhythms. For ninety minutes you will typically be engaged in whatever activity you wish to be engaged in. After this ninety minutes has passed you start to daydream and slip out of consciousness and into hypnosis. This state is one when you feel yourself thinking about things outside of what you should be focused on consciously. Maybe you're thinking about what you're going to have for dinner, or what you're going to do when you get home after work in the evening, and you're even going to be making up fantasies that have not yet occurred, and probably will not happen in your outside world, in their truest sense of what we label 'reality'. For example, we might envision ourselves doing something different professionally than what we are actually doing professionally (during this ultradian rest period). Maybe we are embellishing our existence by focusing on more of what we want as opposed to what we currently have. This is perfectly natural, and everyone does it. When you find yourself, however, feeling depressed or not as driven to succeed as you would like to be, you can apply the same hypnosis induction taught in this chapter to help you refocus your mind back onto an earlier period in the day when you felt more energized, focused, and excited about what the day had in store for you. This can greatly increase your excitement levels emotionally in the present sense, so you can create for yourself a better outcome for today. So I guess what I'm trying to get at here is you can look back on a past experience from way back when, or you can very simply look at a period of time today (earlier) when you felt more resourceful, and using this hypnosis induction apply it to how you're feeling currently, so you can contrast what the differences are and what you might need to do in terms of your emotional well-being to get you back to a more resourceful state of mind and feeling happy and goal focused.

CONCLUSION

In this chapter you learned about a self-hypnosis induction that had you comparing where you are now in your life compared to a time in the past when you felt much more resourceful, confident, and excited about what the future had in store for you. Contrasting these two events and making a mental decision to realign yourself back to an earlier state of resourcefulness can have profound effects in the quality of your life in terms of how you feel and what results you achieve. You also learned why this easy to implement induction can help you in other contexts; such as, improving your day, as the day moves on. You also learned what you need to know up front in order to implement this induction, i.e. sub modalities. Then you learned, of course, the few steps it takes to successfully utilize this hypnosis induction to quickly realize the changes inside you changing so you can be more successful and see the types of outcomes you want to see happening in your life successfully played-out.

In the next chapter we are going to synergize in a sense the previous two inductions and look more closely at how you can adjust your life by isolating certain mental pictures and enhancing those pictures through mental conscious management. In this induction we will actually be looking at fiction aspects of hypnosis specifically a metaphor that can be adopted in order to help us to isolate the empowered and good feelings we want to experience, while diminishing those emotions which are less useful to us. Once your mind has adjusted to these changes the results can be phenomenal. You will likely experience positive change sooner than you think utilizing this very special self-hypnotic induction. So let's get to the learning, shall we?

CHAPTER 9

THE ADJUST YOUR LIFE CONTROL PANEL HYPNOTIC INDUCTION.

INTRODUCTION

In the previous chapter we looked at the advantages of going back in time to previous moments in our life when we felt extremely empowered and hopeful about our futures. By reliving this experience cerebrally it actually causes within us positive emotional changes which are associated and linked to the right types of actions we will take to get us back to where we want to be. In this way, we actually go back in order to move forward. As the adage goes: we take one step forward, but two steps back. In this case, however, taking a step back is more beneficial than trying to wade through the quicksand that is taking us down problematically. We talked about why learning this hypnotic induction was important. We talked about what needed to be understood in terms of sub modalities on the front-end before actually implementing the strategy. I taught you the sequential steps of the induction so that you can quickly and easily apply it yourself, as you like. We looked at how the induction could be utilized simply by going back in our day to a time when we felt more energized and then applying that energy in terms of our feelings to times later in the day when we perhaps feel less energetic and perhaps sluggish.

In this chapter you will be learning The Adjust Your Life Control Panel Induction. This induction uses a hypnotic metaphor in order to empower yourself mentally to adopt changes specifically where you want to adopt them. The metaphor is a *life control panel* in which you control what happens with this imagined machine, which gets transferred over into day-to-day life. This is one of those inductions you may adopt frequently in terms of using it, because in many ways this is a very empowering induction that puts you in control and in the driver's seat of your life. If you ever feel insecure or as if you just can't navigate your path anymore, this induction will help you overcome that useless mentality. You will be discovering how to apply this induction in such a way that you never have to worry about

feeling out of control ever again. I really like this induction. Let me teach it to you.

WHY YOU SHOULD LEARN AND APPLY THE ADJUST OUR LIFE CONTROL PANEL SELF-HYPNOSIS INDUCTION?

I wonder if you realize you are experiencing a particular
mood right now? You can continue right on thinking
about how you feel at this given moment, and as you do
you might think about whether or not the state of mind
you're in right now is a desirable state or a less desirable
state than a mood you may have been in earlier today.
Suppose you did understand where I was going with all
of this? You probably would be able to make more
sense out of my meaning. So let me assure you, sooner
or later you will completely understand the reason why
it is so important you understand this specific self-
hypnosis induction.

You see certain moods help us accomplish more than
what other moods might. This is something so simple,
yet it is something we overlook because it is so obvious.
If you take, for example, a situation in which a parent
tells a child to do their homework and the child answers
back, "But mum, I'm not in the mood!" In this situation
the child is telling the parent they don't *feel* like doing
their homework right now. They are not in the *right*

mood to be motivated enough actually to do their homework. The same thing can be applied to adult situations as well. For example, perhaps you work in a firm and you are expected to accomplish a certain work project by a specific deadline. Assuming that this were the case there would be times you would feel more like working on the project, and there would be other times when you did not feel like working on the project. Have you ever thought about what mood is necessary in order for you to take action and get the work done that is needed to get done? Most people don't! No! Most people tend to go through life without consciously thinking about what motivates them and what does not. Mood and ones feelings have a lot to do with this, once again. People don't take into consideration how they feel moment to moment, and as a result of this they tend not to be able to predict with a high level of likelihood at what juncture they will actually take action and get the work done that they need to get done.

What if I told you that there was a way you could instantly put yourself into the right mood necessary for you to want to actually get done what you need to get done? Suppose I added that there was a way, and that it only required a few moments of your time and a little bit of visualization in order to make it happen? Would you get a little bit excited? If you're like most people, probably you would get a little excited, because I've coached many people in the same technique during live self-hypnosis workshops, and the responses I have received have been nearly all the same; namely, which is, that this self-hypnosis induction has literally changed their lives for the better, forever. Now, dear reader, you know why you should learn this self-hypnosis induction. Let's now turn our attention toward what you need to know up front so you can make this a reality for yourself and begin applying it immediately.

WHAT YOU MUST UNDERSTAND UPFRONT BEFORE YOU CAN APPLY THE ADJUST YOUR LIFE CONTROL PANEL SELF-HYPNOSIS INDUCTION.

There are a few ingredients to making this work. The first ingredient is that you need to be free mentally in order to do a quick visualization technique I will teach you. Let me assure you the technique is very simple and will not take up much of your time whatsoever. The second ingredient in this recipe for success is you must be able to recognize aspects of your inborn nature which tends to be more motivated than other parts of you. Don't be confused by this, because all it simply means is recognizing when you are in a motivated state of mind or mood, and when you are not. Believe me when I tell you, this is all you need to know in order to apply this self-hypnosis induction I'm about to disclose to you. On this note, let's learn how to apply the adjust your life control panel self-hypnosis induction. Let's move on.

HOW TO APPLY THE ADJUST YOUR LIFE CONTROL PANEL SELF-HYPNOSIS INDUCTION?

The following steps are going to teach you methodically exactly how to apply a simple sequence of steps that are going to ensure your success with applying this self-hypnosis induction. I want to strongly encourage you to remember (or better put...*memorize*) this specific sequence, because it is going to transform how you turn on and off your productivity restraints. Whenever you find yourself out of the mood to get done what needs to be done, I want you to think about this hypnosis induction and then apply it when you must. Suddenly, when you do, you will find that you instantly become more motivated and driven to push past the limitations of how you felt just moments earlier before implementing the strategy. With this being said let's move right into how to actually apply this induction. Here we go.

INDUCTION #7 - ADJUST YOUR LIFE CONTROL PANEL

1. Step 1 - Once you've reached a particular mood or emotional level that serves you well, enhance the effectiveness of this mood by picturing your emotions as a control panel.

2. Step 2 - Isolate the aspects of your current mood you wish to increase while also isolating certain emotions you wish to decrease.

3. Step 3 - Closing your eyes, grab hold of the dials for each of these emotions. Adjust the intensity of each emotion by turning the dial and visually seeing the indicator rise or fall as you see fit.

4. Step 4 - Open your eyes and continue with your newly adjusted mind.

HOW ELSE MIGHT THIS APPLY TO OTHER CONTEXTS BESIDES MOTIVATION?

For starters you can apply this simple hypnosis induction to other areas using the same basic framework—memorizations, focus, charisma, and so forth. The sky is the limit. However, like everything in life, it's easier said than done. Even so, keep in your mind that it is not difficult to apply, as it's only four tiny little steps that a child could probably do, and might even do better than most adults. Children have wild imaginations, don't they? This aside, you can do this, and you can apply it to nearly anything in your life you want to improve upon.

I personally like motivation, because it is state dependent. Speaking of state dependent learning, you can also train your brain to focus more intentionally whenever you mentally revisit this self-hypnosis induction and modify it for a focus context.

When I was a child my mother gave me a similar approach in which I was to imagine an imaginary friend giving me the answers to math problems I was supposed to memorize, but couldn't. I got them all right, and I didn't even know a one. "How?" you ask? The answer is: Through the power of the principle behind this hypnosis induction. Don't take my word for it however, instead apply it and test its efficacy for yourself.

CONCLUSION

In this chapter we covered *The Adjust Your Life Control Panel Self-Hypnosis Induction.* Keep in mind that you should assume at this point you will utilize your capabilities as a hypnotist now to put yourself into a trance state. Once you have achieved this you will then apply the inductions in this book (e.g., Adjust Your Life Control Panel Induction). This induction, we have said, is great for dispersing the negative factors that hold you back from success, while increasing the positive aspects of yourself which serve to carry you further in life. A simple mental exercise has incredible power to bolster your capabilities, make you shine, and help you succeed where many will stray. You learned how to implement this powerful metaphor so your hypnotic mind could make associations with and bring about outwardly in your life what you seek and wish for your life to look like. You also are encouraged to take some time and think about other ways you can utilize this technique to help you self-improve other areas of your life. I should note, at this point, that the idea of 'utilization' is not a new one in indirect hypnosis applications. Whenever you can, get in the habit of utilizing things you find in your environment to help assist you entering trance. By letting yourself adjust to working in trance states you'll discover you get so much more done effortlessly. Effort is perceived (becoming mentally real) when the conscious mind interferes with the natural ebb and flow of the hypnotic mind's ability to process ideas. Sometimes all that is required is that you get out of the way and let things naturally flow. This is the nature and power of hypnosis. This being said, make sure you always play it safe with hypnosis and never intentionally put yourself in jeopardy by being hypnotized when you're operating any type of machinery or driving your vehicle.

In the next chapter we will investigate The Confronting Negative Habits Induction. This powerful self-hypnosis induction will help you to get rid of habits that are robbing you of success and prosperity, health and wellness, and other areas of your life that are being infringed upon due to your propensity to repeat events over and over again expecting to get a different result. You should learn these inductions if you want to self-improve and overcome obstacles that may be holding you back. What you'll need to do is simply follow the instructions I'll be presenting to you and be on the

lookout mentally for possible habits that may unconsciously be holding you back. Let's move along now and
learn what this induction is and how it can help you.

CHAPTER 10

THE CONFRONTING NEGATIVE HABITS INDUCTION

INTRODUCTION

In this previous chapter you learned how to get more of what you want and less of what you don't; in a matter of speaking. You learned that the hypnotic mind makes associations with metaphors and examples that it relates back and helps to improve parts of yourself you need work on. You can visualize, imagine hearing, and even consider what turning those two knobs might feel like— all in your mind. When you do this your hypnotic mind takes what you imagine and runs with it to help you improve aspects of your life that you feel need some improvement.

In this chapter we'll look at the effects of negative habits and how they play a role in holding you back, possibly losing for us *competitive advantage*, and what can be done to correct these habits so we rebalance our lives and get back on track so we can move closer toward our goals. This induction will have you confronting these habits so you can break down these walls and rebuild them with new positive and helpful habits. When you apply this self-hypnosis induction you are validating to yourself you want to self-improve and are willing to take the necessary steps, i.e. face your limitations, so that you can deal with the problems and make mental corrections so that outwardly you function more prosperously. Your life path is going to see positive changes once again, when you implement this pattern of using hypnosis regularly to self-improve. I'm excited for you. Let's learn, okay?

WHY YOU SHOULD LEARN THE CONFRONTING NEGATIVE HABITS INDUCTION?

Let me preface by saying that habits are neither good nor bad in and of themselves. Some habits, however, do us more good than others which do us more harm. Now this may sound like I'm saying one thing and then advocating quite another. On the other hand a habit is simply a repetition of something that is done either of the conscious level or the unconscious level. Now personally, I look at the unconscious mind as the hypnotic mind, or what I sometimes will refer to as the other mind, but most people are familiar with the conscious mind in the subconscious mind, so just be aware of this as you go throughout this book. You can consciously decide that every day you're going to do an activity, and by continually doing this activity you are consciously making a habit of doing something repetitively. Whatever you decide to do repetitively is up to you, and for this reason you are in control of your choice to do it or not to do it. If, for example, you decided that every day when you woke up you're going to do some type of spiritual exercise to help you feel closer to God, then this exercise, depending on how you look at it, could be perceived as a positive force for good in your life, or a potential negative. This all goes back to the glass half full and the glass half empty analogy. For some people making a habit of doing something will be perceived as a positive at first, yet perhaps much later as time progresses they may perceive it as a negative which they no longer resonate with. So this goes back to what I prefaced with, which is habits in and of them are neither good nor bad per se. You want to do with habits is isolate them, identify whether or not they are helping you or hurting you, so that you can decide for yourself if this is a bad habit or if it is a positive habit. Once you have determined this, you are then freed up to do what is needed to help you self-improve and move closer toward the direction you wish for your life to head.

The primary reason why you need to understand and know the confronting negative habits.induction is because it's going to assist you with aligning all the aspects of yourself with the final destination you have in mind which is that place which you perceived to be the completion of a goal or as some would call it a dream. Going back to I said before, if you change what your dream is where your goal is the habits that you have in place now may very well and in all likelihood need to be changed or eliminated even in order for you to change directions and move in a new direction toward a new goal. The goals that may have been perceived of as positive and useful when you had a different objective in mind in terms of your goals and where you want your life to head, may now need to be changed or altered slightly to reflect what is needed now to get you closer to your new dreams or new goal. So for this reason I urge you to keep an open mind about habits, and not to judge yourself too harshly for whatever habits you happen to have acquired. Some people reading this, may think that smoking is a bad habit. For some people reading this they may perceive smoking is being a good habit, because it helps them in some way function mentally and emotionally and so forth. Now, don't get me wrong,; I'm not advocating that smoking is good for you in terms of its health benefits, but what I am saying is the habit of smoking may have been put in place at some point in your life to help you cope so that you could move closer toward an outcome you desired to achieve. For this reason, again, don't beat yourself up about your habits, trust me, they can be changed.

WHAT DO YOU NEED TO KNOW UP FRONT IN ORDER TO BE ABLE TO CHANGE A HABIT USING THE CONFRONTING NEGATIVE HABITS INDUCTION?

So perhaps you are already aware of some of the habits you have, yet there's a good possibility that you may not be aware of all of your habits which may be holding you back from achieving what it is you want to achieve in life. This hypnotic induction is going to help you discover what habits you have so that you can work toward isolating the ones that no longer work for you any longer, while installing new habits that are going to help you move your life closer toward your goals and dreams. So the first thing you should know is habits are neither good nor bad, as they serve certain usefulness and uselessness. The second thing you need to understand before implementing this induction is that it is going to require an upfront willingness to want to change habits that are no longer working for you, while installing habits that will help you achieve the types of outcomes you want to achieve. The last thing you really need to understand is some outcomes may be perceived by others to be negative, while to other people they may be perceived to be as positives. For this reason, it is important to understand that what matters most is how you perceive a goal or outcome to be in terms of its usefulness and benefits to you personally. Some people are definitely going to judge what you want to achieve as ridiculous and useless, while other people are going to be supporters and encouragers for you along your journey. The main thing to realize is you don't have to share your goals with everyone. You can choose to share your goals with those individuals in your life who are the most supportive and who will be the most helpful in supporting and holding you accountable for achieving what it is you want to achieve. There is no greater feeling in my opinion than achieving something that you've set a goal for yourself to achieve. The sense of accomplishment one gains is helpful and inspiring to make us want to carry on and achieve other things in life. This constant progression of achieving one thing and then moving on to another thing makes for an exciting and interesting life in my opinion. Change is definitely a constant, and so for this reason we should learn to embrace change and accept that we are in control of our own lives and have the power within us to hypnotically change anything.

HOW TO IMPLEMENT THE CONFRONTING NEGATIVE HABITS INDUCTION

This induction is no less easy than any of the others you've learnt so far. It does require you to let yourself relax and get comfortable, and then to do some internal visualization. Keep in mind why you want to apply this induction, what areas (habits) you hope to correct to best suit your life path, and think in terms of mindfulness and being in the present. Let yourself be hypnotized and then proceed with these steps.

INDUCTION #8 - CONFRONTING NEGATIVE HABITS

1. Step 1 - Position yourself in a way that's most comfortable and eliminate all external distractions, such as the computer, television or music.

2. Step 2 - Close your eyes and take 10 deep breaths. Upon the 10th breath, open your mind and begin filtering through habits that must require changing.

3. Step 3 - Isolate each habit one-by-one. See this habit. Feel it through your mind. Confront the reality of what this habit does to your mind and body and how it negatively effects your life path.

4. Step 4 - Speak to this habit, either vocally or internally, and dissect its properties. Determine that this habit has no use in your life or mind.

5. Step 5 - Imagine deconstructing the habit one element at a time. Instead of leaving an empty space where it once was, fill it with a new habit. One that truly benefits your life.

HOW ELSE MIGHT YOU THINK ABOUT THIS INDUCTION IN TERMS OF IT HELPING YOU SPECIFICALLY TO ADOPT USEFUL HABITS, WHILE ELIMINATING HABITS WHICH HINDER YOUR LIFE PATH?

Now that you've learned how to take advantage of this induction and use it to lessen habits which are not useful, while installing new habits which are going to help you immensely, it's now time to think about the application and implications of using this self-hypnosis induction. I think it's interesting to ask ourselves the question what if? When we do this we start to brainstorm and see opportunities for utilizing information in ways we may not have noticed consciously before. My getting her head sometimes and thinking about how we can solve problems and what we can do to prosper our lives, we start to come up with solutions that are golden. For this reason I want to encourage you with this induction to take a few moments now, and think about how this is going to impact your life, but also how you can apply it to other goals you may have, then the one you have probably been thinking about all along now. It also helps to chunk down your thoughts into specifics. In other words, if you happen to be reading this book and you perceive this induction theoretically, meaning that you have not considered how to help yourself in one particular way or another, the now is the time for you to think about some of the areas of your life you want to improve, and how this specific hypnotic language induction is going to help you get there.

CONCLUSION

In this chapter you learned a self-hypnosis induction that can be utilized to help you overcome habits which are no longer working for you, so you can install new habits which are going to help and prosper the direction you want to go in life. You learned why this induction was important to understand, and why it's important to understand the nature of a habit, instead of just judging a habit is being either good or bad. Keeping an open mind can be quite helpful in allowing change to happen naturally. He also learned what you needed to understand on the front and in terms of implementing this specific hypnotic induction. And finally you learned the induction, and were given the opportunity to think about some different ways that this hypnotic induction is going to help you. You also were given instruction to start chunking down what your goals are in terms of specifics, so that you can now begin to think about what habits will be useful, in which habits well maybe not work any longer.

In the next chapter you will be learning how to identify the reality of a situation; sort of like how we lose our sense of understanding about certain situations we perceive as reality. The honest truth is 'meaning' is sometimes lost in communication. When meaning is lost in communication people tend to think one dimensionally one thing, though the actual reality or intention of the other person communicating with you may have been quite a different case altogether. In many ways, this next induction, which is called *The Identity By The Reality Of Situations Self-Hypnosis Induction*, is going to help you become more mindful of the world around you so you can live in a more positive and peaceful world (whatever that means to you), where you're more in tune of your feelings and emotions so you can regain control of your life by objectively looking at your physical surroundings and how those surroundings affect your moods and how you perceive reality to be. A metaphor I like to use, as this is concerned, has to do with the way that you perceive things as a child. Perhaps your first home, for example. Years later after being after having become a grownup, you travel back to the same house you grew-up in, and you realize the home was actually much smaller than what you once perceived it to be. And again, what seems huge to a child may seem quite small to an adult who has had more opportunities to contrast sizes of homes by comparing those to other houses they have experienced since childhood. The idea here, with this induction, is to help you become more mindful and able to identify certain situations that may have caused you to flare up with certain emotions, which aren't normal to your everyday make up. So with all this in mind, let's move forward, and let's learn exactly what this induction is all about. Let's go!

THE IDENTITY BY THE REALITY OF SITUATIONS SELF-HYPNOSIS INDUCTION

INTRODUCTION

In the previous chapter we talked about the importance of looking at your habits objectively and deciding, depending on where you are at this point in your life, what habits are ones you want to keep, and which habits do you need to let go of. It's important to take stock of what you do regularly. A habit in and of itself is something we do regularly—an activity. My point is, it is important to look at habit-patterns, in order to assess the aspects of our daily routines we need to let go of, and possible adoption of routines, which will assist us on our life path. We want more of what brings us closer into alignment with our goals; while, less of what keeps us from our goals.

In this chapter we turn our focus over to the practicalities of the here and now, which is where our focus sometimes needs to be. We get caught up in our mind by emotion and the interplay of thought-patterns that continue to loop and create unintended problems for us. Specifically, we will be looking at reality in relationship to our external environment. You need to be able to look at what's going on around you, so you can remain present and in the here and now. Thinking too much about the past or too much about the future may cause you to dissociate from your present, which is where you always are right now in your life. And again, there's nothing wrong with looking at the future or reflecting on the path past from time to time, because it shows us where we've been, and helps us to track and stay abreast of where we are actually going.

For the sake of this chapter, you'll be experiencing an induction that will help you to let go of emotional baggage that is con founding your journey, so that you can relinquish some of the emotional stress and anxiety that is brained on your energy level. Just like if where we are too physical we tend to tire ourselves out bodily, the mind has a tendency also to become so busy that mentally we become weary and lose our cognitive ability to think hardheadedly. The key thing to remember here is there's always room for improvement. If you've gotten to this induction, and you don't feel like it will serve you well, just consider for a moment all the things going on in your life, and how often you tend to think about what you don't have, or what you wish was different, and so on. So with that said, let's turn our attention now over to *The Identify The Reality Of Situations Self-Hypnosis Induction.*

WHY IS THE IDENTIFY THE REALITY OF SITUATIONS SELF-HYPNOSIS INDUCTION AN IMPORTANT ONE FOR HELPING YOU TO STAY FOCUSED ON WHAT'S IMPORTANT IN YOUR EVERYDAY REALITY?

Most of the things we think about and fear never come to pass. The problem is, the very act of thinking about these fear thoughts cause anxiety and stress to well up within our beings. For this reason it is important to understand this hypnosis induction, because it's going to allow you to look let go of and refocus your thoughts on to things that actually matter. This is important for your personal development. More so, you can also help other people after understanding this hypnosis induction, so that they themselves can gain the benefits of this hypnosis induction as well.

WHAT DO YOU NEED TO UNDERSTAND IN ORDER TO IMPLEMENT THE IDENTIFY THE REALITY OF SITUATIONS SELF-HYPNOSIS INDUCTION?

Firstly, you have to understand that most of the time when we are thinking these thoughts that don't really relate to our everyday reality or situations, that we are not aware that we are actually looping these thoughts over and over in our minds. For many of us these thoughts and ideas revolve so frequently, that they wear us down, and cause us to feel sluggish, lose our energy, and fall into a routine they can actually cause us to become depressed. It's important to understand on the front and, before implementing this self-hypnosis induction that sometimes we don't know why we feel the way we feel, given how great our lives happen to be. We all have heard people tell us that there depressed, and when we evaluate their life we think ourselves quiet in the world is this person depressed; they have everything. So, this self-hypnosis induction is going to help you discover the things going on inside of you emotionally that have become formed habits, which are in turn going to help you to alleviate some of these emotions that no longer work for you any longer, so that you can move on and move past them so that you can begin enjoying your life once again. I think it's time now to learn the induction. So let's do that.

HOW TO IMPLEMENT THE IDENTIFY THE REALITY OF SITUATIONS SELF-HYPNOSIS INDUCTION FOR ULTIMATE EFFECTIVENESS?

Taking action is one of the most challenging aspects of most anything. You get a good idea in your head, and what do most people do? The answer is they lose the idea quickly to yet another idea. For this reason it is important to remain reticent by not sharing your ideas with everyone, before taking some action(s) in the right direction. Your follow-through must be there for you to be successful with most opportunities in life. The ability to take action supersedes the theory in principle; in my opinion. The following steps will help you to take action immediately and achieve some benefits. You may want to keep a journal when applying this self-help self-hypnosis induction. Writing down your thoughts and feelings will help to clear space for healing to happen.

INDUCTION #9 - IDENTIFY THE REALITY OF SITUATIONS

1. Step 1 - Eliminate the influence of issues and situations that don't actually affect your physical reality by focusing your attention on this internal   feeling.

2. Step 2 - Isolate the situation that caused this emotion to flare. Breakdown the phone call, in-person conversation or actions that this emotion uses as its foundation. Recount what happened, but instead of viewing it as a reality, view it for what it actually is - an internal element.

3. Step 3 - Focus on the world around you; the physical world. Instruct your mind to let go of the negative feelings and emotions and regain control by basing its current mood on the physical surroundings of your reality.

HOW ELSE CAN IMPLEMENTING THE IDENTIFY THE REALITY OF SITUATIONS SELF-HYPNOSIS INDUCTION HELP YOU IN OTHER WAYS YOU MAY NOT HAVE CONSIDERED YET?

So now that you know how to implement this induction for yourself, let's think about some of the other ways that applying this self-hypnosis induction and self-therapy is going to help you outside of the immediate situation. When you have more energy you will find that the activities you take on in your external reality become more meaningful and cause you to feel more whole within your being. You're also going to feel empowered, because you will now know how to isolate those situations which have caused the emotions inside of you to flare up. Finally, you're going to be able to more enjoy the life you have before you. When you're able to enjoy life to its fullest you are able to bring more value to other people in your external reality as well.

CONCLUSION

In this chapter we looked at a very special self-hypnosis induction called the *Identify The Reality Of Situations.* You learned that this induction begins with eliminating the influence that certain issues and situations which don't actually affect your physical reality have on you internally. When you look at how you feel on the inside and can isolate certain situations which have caused you to feel this way it helps you to realize that this is really not something that affects you outside of your mental state; rather, it's merely an internal element which is causing you distress. The key thing you learned is to focus on the world around you. This means looking at the world in terms of what you see is what you get. Any types of negative feelings or emotions that you housed within you can be let go of utilizing this simple to implement self-hypnosis induction. You also learn the importance of why you should care about applying this induction, which has to do with you living in the present and not backtracking to the past mentally or being so focused on your future that you don't enjoy the journey that you're on.

In the next chapter we will look at a new induction. The induction we will look at is called the *Transcend To Tranquility Induction.* As the name suggests you will actually be moving from the state of mind that you are in currently to a place of tranquility, peace, and relaxation. This is a fun induction, because of the visual aspects which incorporate a dry erase board in your mind, in order for you to have power over all the things going on in your life. Whenever you want to get rid of certain elements in your life that you perceive as of being negative or which complicate how productive you are, you will be able to implement this easy self-hypnosis induction and quickly gain the benefits of eradicating all negativity. Sometimes we tend to think about imaginary scenarios, which can actually cause a stress, anxiety, and even depression. Sometimes we get to a point in our life where we become unable to control these types of thoughts and impulses that mentally affect us and cause us to behave outside the norms of society. This simple hypnosis induction will help you feel whole, peaceful, and *at one* with the world, once again. With this being said, let's turn our attention now over to the next chapter, and find out exactly how to implement this special self-hypnosis induction.

THE TRANSCEND TO TRANQUILITY INDUCTION

INTRODUCTION

In the previous chapter we talked about how sometimes your internal thoughts and emotional well-being can affect your perceptions in terms of the outside world around you. With the induction that you learned; namely, identify the reality of the situation, you learned that this induction starts by having you eliminate certain influences which hold power over certain issues and situations which in fact do not actually affect your physical reality. They do on the other hand, however, affect you mentally. When you have a lot going on inside your head it's often difficult for you to enjoy being in the present moment, and for this reason this specific induction is useful for helping you get outside of your head and back into the outside world around you.

In the next chapter in this chapter we will be exploring a brand-new self-hypnosis induction called the Transcend to tranquility induction. This induction is one of the more fun inductions, in my opinion. I say this because this induction gives you the opportunity to creatively use a mental dry erase board where you have control of the markers and the dry erase pad in order to give you complete rain over your thoughts and annihilate negativity while increasing productivity. I have always liked the idea of using creative tools such as art, or in this case the use of the dry erase board in order to make understanding complex ideas more easier. I think you're really going to embrace this self-hypnosis induction, because it actually is something that you will be able to relate with, and usually when someone is using a dry erase board it means that they are in control as they are typically the ones giving a presentation. In this case you get the opportunity to present to yourself what you need and what you do not so that you can make the appropriate changes and get to a resource state that is going to help you along your life path.

WHY SHOULD YOU LEARN THE TRANSCEND TO TRANQUILITY SELF-HYPNOSIS INDUCTION?

The easiest ways to explain something is to utilize a resource tool such as a dry erase board. In life everyday stresses can pile up and irritate us to the point we just want to bury our heads in the ground and leave the world behind. So that this does not happen it's advisable that you utilize certain self-therapies such as hypnotherapy in order to create a life for yourself that is a worry free and stress-free. Sure there's always going to be certain levels of conflict which come into our lives, but it is a way that you handle such conflicts which will determine how successful you are and how quickly you ascertain your goals in life. In hypnosis sometimes you have to go slow in order to go fast. By allowing yourself to relax, which may seem like a counterproductive idea where as productivity is relate to, you actually put yourself into a state of mind, i.e. hypnotic state, which actually makes productivity effortless. In other words, you are going to be reaping some huge rewards as a result of letting yourself and her this tranquil and peaceful relaxation.

WHAT DO YOU NEED TO KNOW UP FRONT SO THAT YOU CAN PROPERLY IMPLEMENT AND DO THE TRANSCEND TO TRANQUILITY SELF-HYPNOSIS INDUCTION?

When you internalize an idea in your mind it is important to utilize your five senses to paint an in-depth and rich picture to make your imagination as real as possible. The first thing you need to understand about this hypnosis induction, and I would even go so far as to say most hypnosis inductions, is that you need to be fully engaged in pay full attention to your relaxation, your body, and most importantly the instructions you give yourself. With this self-hypnosis induction you are going to be visualizing yourself at a whiteboard, where you have full access to all kinds of different colored dry erase markers, but also the dry race server itself. You're free to explore whatever you want to explore with this dry erase board. When you start to see images appear on this dry erase board that are negative and useless to you today, you have the capability in your mind to erase those forever, so that you can make room on the board for new experiences and statements about what it is you want. You're also free to let yourself relax and enter a tranquil state so that whatever instructions you decide you need you can be sure that they take affect and become implanted on the walls of your hypnotic mind.

HOW TO DO THE TRANSCEND TO TRANQUILITY SELF-HYPNOSIS INDUCTION?

This induction may seem like more steps, but trust me, once you apply it and practice it a time or two through, you'll see it as very easy to implement. The rewards of this induction are amazing, plus it's a good time (in my opinion). Let's learn the steps now.

INDUCTION #10 - TRANSCEND TO TRANQUILITY

1. Step 1 - Imagine the world around you as a dry erase board, and you have control of the markers and eraser.

2. Step 2 - Begin erasing elements in your life that bring you negativity or complicate your productivity.

3. Step 3 - Once these images are erased, begin drawing images that bring you true peace, tranquility and confidence. These can be previous experiences or imaginary scenarios. Allow these situations to become your current reality. Em-

brace the physical sensations of these imaginary images and situations.

HOW ELSE CAN THIS SIMPLE INDUCTION EXERCISE HELP YOU IN OTHER WAYS AS WELL?

The first thing that comes to my mind, when I think about this induction and how else it can be utilized to help me personally, I think about memory. When you have the ability to imagine a dry erase board in your mind, giving yourself free axis and rain to write or draw on it whatever you want, just knowing that you can visualize this board anytime you want, will allow you to access memories, or anything else you want to remember by simply drawing it on the board and being able to recall it later at will. Of course there are many other applications in which this specific induction can help you, but at this time I would like to leave it up to you to come up with a few on your own. When you do, you can be assured that you are empowered even more. And, again, you want to start thinking outside the box and crafting ideas in your mind in terms of how these inductions are going to start helping you for your unique contexts. If you've been practicing the inductions throughout this book thus far, by now you're becoming an expert at self-hypnosis. You're learning about the benefits of self-hypnosis, and your applying self-hypnosis in a way that is fundamentally going to change her life for the best. When you start to know that you are in control of your own future, by simply communicating with your hypnotic mind whatever instructions you wish for it to carry out for you, it basically takes a lot of pressure off of your conscious mind, allowing you to live a more peaceful and tranquil existence.

CONCLUSION

In this chapter you learned one of my favorite self-hypnosis inductions. It's my favorite, because it's in my opinion the most fun. This induction consists of you being able to write whatever you want as well as the race what you draw on a mental dry erase board. In the process of caring fourth this induction, you are also entering a deep state of relaxation and tranquility. The act of being able to relax is difficult for many people, because they've become comfortable with being uncomfortable, and this is robbing them every single day of their life from complete joy and fulfillment. It rubs off into other areas of their life as well, which has a profound impact on whether or not they will ever be able to accomplish their goals and dreams. I want the absolute best for you, and for this reason I want you to apply the self-hypnosis induction in a way that works best for you, and apply it so that when you're finished you have absolute certainty and knowing that the instructions you've given your hypnotic mind will be carried out.

In the next chapter we are going to explore one final self-hypnosis induction. Namely, *The Throw Away Stress Self Hypnosis Induction.* At first, this self-hypnosis induction may seem counterintuitive; considering it actually has you first begin accumulating both physical stress and emotional stress within your mind. The reality, however, is that as you imagine and bring to your awareness the stresses that you have, you will be able to literally, just as you would with ice cream, scoop out this stress and get rid of it forever. So much of your stress, leaving your body and your mind, is dependent on your willingness to let go of it. Many people do become attached to their feelings of anxiety. Some people use their own stress as a crutch for why they give away their power to others. Some people use stress as a logical explanation for why they have lost self-confidence in their own abilities to achieve in life the goals they've always wanted to realize. Get ready to close your eyes and enter one of the deepest hypnotic trances you've ever experienced. Let's hop on over to the next chapter, and discover more, shall we?

CHAPTER 13

THE THROW AWAY THE STRESS INDUCTION

INTRODUCTION

In the previous chapter you learned one of my favorite self-hypnosis inductions, which involves using a mental dry erase board along with dry erase markers and a dry eraser for wiping away things that no longer resonate with you in your life while adding new resources and brainstorming about the things that you do want and would like to see happen in your life. I can't underscore enough how much fun this induction has been for me over the years. When I think back on many of my accomplishments in life I can attribute much of that success to the induction that I shared with you.

In this chapter I'm going to give you one final self-hypnosis induction which I think can be applied immediately right out of the gates. I have intentionally saved this 11th induction for the very end of this book, because I assumed that many of you reading this book would first read the book one time through and I wanted this last induction to actually be the first induction that you utilized for yourself. The reason I wanted you to utilize this induction first is because it's going to help you to de-stress and eliminate much of the anxiety that can hold people back from having a pleasant self-hypnosis experience.

One of the things I really enjoy about this specific hypnotic induction is it has a built in metaphor which I believe most people can identify with. This metaphor is a stress ball. It wasn't too many years ago that I was teaching a hypnotic sales training course at a Fortune 500 telecommunications company in Southwest Florida. While I was teaching this course one of the initiatives of the program was that students would eventually get on the phones and begin making sales calls. Many of the students in my class had never sold anything professionally at any time in their lives. It was my job to make sure that when it was time for them to get on the phones that they were well-prepared and could successfully sell ice to Eskimos, so to speak. One of the things that these call center representatives were all given, which surprised me even, were stress balls. The stress balls were foam balls that would fit in the palm of a person's hands and allow them to quickly pump the foam balls in order to release anxiety and stress as well as frustration when they would be talking to potential customers on the phone and having a hard go at it. When you give someone a stress ball it almost presupposes that stress is eminent in that profession. I'm still not quite sure how I feel about that company freely giving over the stress balls to their call center representatives, but I do suspect that some good did come from it and it did help the sales professionals to have an outlet for venting their frustrations without it affecting their calls.

With this in mind, please keep in mind that this special self-hypnosis induction is going to essentially do what the stress balls did was call center representatives. It's going to allow you to let go of unwanted stress, and even stress that you may have been holding onto because of some attachment to it. Let's start learning.

WHY LEARN THIS THROW AWAY THE STRESS SELF-HYPNOSIS INDUCTION?

This election is going to do several things for you. The first thing is going to do is give you an outlet for your stress while at the same time helping you to replace stress with positive thoughts and attitudes. The second thing it's going to do for you is help you to become a better self-hypnosis subject. By this, I simply mean that once you finish utilizing this specific self-hypnosis induction you will be able to more easily slip into trance without any real effort on your part. In fact, truth be told, there shouldn't be any effort whatsoever when it comes to relaxing and letting yourself drift down deep into a nice hypnotic trance. When you are able to let yourself go and experience the wonderment of self-hypnosis and the benefits that come along with incorporating it into your everyday life you will first hand understand why so many top-performing professionals use it every single day of their lives. The more you can experience self-hypnosis the more you can experience it. And again, it only takes a little bit of your time each day in order to experience the very real benefits that it brings to you. After you through utilizing this specific self-hypnosis induction you will feel more relaxed and better about life and excited about the prospect of what can happen and come about as a result of you implementing this self-hypnosis induction.

WHAT SHOULD YOU HAVE IN YOUR HEAD FIRST BEFORE LEARNING HOW TO IMPLEMENT THE THROW AWAY STRESS INDUCTION?

So, to begin with, you need to find out what's been holding you back from success. Finding this out is going to require that you introspect some, which in itself can be quite hypnotic. You also need to be able to suspend your doubt in disbelief in order to be receptive and embracing of this hypnotic induction. The most important aspect of implementing any self-hypnosis induction is your attitude toward self-hypnosis. If you would ask 100 people what they thought of hypnosis you would invariably get a broad range of answers from those people. The reason for this is because some people have certain doubts about hypnosis, while other people who have experienced hypnosis firsthand will give you quite a different perspective altogether. For this reason it's important to keep an open mind. It doesn't matter what you've heard from other people, all that matters is that you trust yourself and trust in the process. Every single day of your life you enter into multiple hypnotic trances. When you're in hypnosis you are not even aware that your hypnotized, which is part of the paradox of hypnosis. As you begin to lie down and relax and let yourself space out and truly relax and focus inwardly on these inductions, this one in particular, you will soon find that hypnosis is one of the easiest things in the world to implement and gain benefit from.

HOW TO IMPLEMENT SUCCESSFULLY THE THROW AWAY THE STRESS SELF-HYPNOSIS INDUCTION?

Implementing anything takes time and patience. What's interesting is it doesn't have to take much of your time or patience implementing this self-hypnosis induction. It is a simple induction to implement. The more you practice implementing it the easier it will be to implement. In time it will be as natural as breathing for you. You'll also have reduced your stress to such an extent you will more rapidly fall under the spell of hypnosis. Let's implement this induction now.

INDUCTION #11 - THROW AWAY STRESS

1. Step 1 - In a comfortable and relaxed state, begin accumulating physical and emotional stress within your mind. Imagine you hold a giant scoop and with every internal dip, you filter stress and anxiety into its net.

2. Step 2 - Imagine the accumulated stress is placed into a compactor. Using all your mental powers,

activate this compactor and begin shrinking stress into a manageable ball.

3. Step 3 - Once the compactor has completed its duty, pick up this stress ball. Look at it, imagine everything that's in there. Become willing to let go of this stress. Many become attached to their feelings of anxiety. Only continue once you're committed to truly eliminating your stress.

4. Step 4 - Moving forward with this confidence, throw this ball of stress into space - to never re-turn. Keeping your eyes closed, rest in the absence of this stress.

5. Step 5 - Begin replacing the spaces where this stress lived with positivity and optimism. Con-tinue until you feel true peace and confidence, which is only present in the absence of stress/anxiety.

HOW ELSE CAN UTILIZING THIS SPECIFIC SELF-HYPNOSIS INDUCTION HELP VARIOUS AREAS OF YOUR LIFE?

Right now you're already beginning to think about the various applications of how self-hypnosis can be suc-cessfully applied to benefit your life. What you're not likely focusing on his the indirect benefits that come as a result of engaging in self-hypnosis regularly. These secondary and tertiary benefits seem to run off into areas of your life that you don't normally focus on that much. From my own experiences I can tell you that the benefits have always been more than what my expectation of those benefits would be. The reason for this is because our minds tend to focus only on 7+ or -2 bits of information at any given moment. When we're taking time to think about how self-hypnosis can help us, often we're limited by our conscious mind's ability to come up with ideas. These ideas will come, nonetheless. They will come at times in your life when you least expect it. It's a good thing to go into hypnosis regularly. It's a good thing to let your hypnotic mind help you in ways your conscious mind does not. I want you now to just think about some of the different areas of your life that this induction will help you. Think about how alleviating stress in your life is going to free up your mind to become more creative and inspired to do things you may otherwise not do. Finally, I want to challenge you to use this self-hypnosis induction for the next 20 days and journal what impact it has on your life. By journaling I mean both how you feel as a result of the self-hypnosis experience as well as how it benefits you indirectly through the insights you gain day in and day out for this 20 day period.

CONCLUSION

In this chapter you learned an important self-hypnosis induction. You learned how to eradicate stress from your emotional makeup as well as your physical makeup. You learn how to reduce stress mentally by forming it into a tiny ball by envisioning a trash compactor, compacting your stress into this smaller form. By having your stress in such a small form you have been given the opportunity to look at your stress and to assess for yourself once and for all why you no longer need to hang onto it. You learn that sometimes people have a tendency to attach themselves to their stress just like their stress attaches to them. There are many other things you can become attached to that will have a more positive impact on your life than stress. When you let go stress you'll find that many of your habits which are useless start to go by the wayside. For example, you may find that you eat due to stress related issues, and now that you no longer have the stress you start to eat more moderate portions and not eat as a result of emotional instability. In this way it helps you buy you losing weight so that you achieve your ideal weight, but also to help you achieve a more nutritious diet that will help you with your own vitality and well-being.

CHAPTER 14

AUTHOR'S NOTES

It has taken me a long time to write this book. Sometimes I can write a book in a day, while other times it takes me many months, and sometimes even years. I have written numerous books, and I must say this is a very special book, because I feel as though I have finally been able to state what I needed to state in order to help people with taking up this regular practice of self-hypnosis. I believe regular practice is going to assist you in ways you can't even imagine, yet. I also believe if you will practice these inductions they will help you with your own personal development, which will lead to higher career advancement, as well as help you in other areas of your life—relationships, health and nutrition, your ability to focus, and to memorize things better. As well, there are a whole host of other things you can't even yet imagine which will happen as a result also.

As a hypnotist I have found that many hypnotists before me have written a book on self-hypnosis before writing any other book on hypnosis. This is been the inverse experience for I myself. This book has come after having written numerous books on hypnosis and neurolinguistic programming, because I wanted my self-hypnosis book to be something special and unique and which would help the people not just overcome a fear or a phobia, but actually be applied in such a general extent that it would help them indirectly correct so many other areas of their life besides one specific problem area. I don't like taking Band-Aid approaches to problem solving. Instead, I like to take approaches which are going to help people dynamically improve their life overall. In this broad sense of how self-hypnosis can be applied, I have done my due diligence and given you the *best of the best* of the inductions I have personally come up with in order that you might appreciate self-hypnosis on your terms, and in the ways that work best for you.

I am really excited for you owning this book. I've read numerous self-hypnosis books, and have been a student of many well-known hypnotists since the time I was a small child. One thing I haven't found in any book I've read on self-hypnosis is how to apply it in a way that not only benefits one area of a person's life, but which will also indirectly improve various other areas of a person's life. This holistic approach to self-hypnosis is very important to me. It's one thing to fix a problem, it's quite another to fix a person. I believe with my heart that if you will follow these inductions and put them to work for yourself that you will revolutionize the way think, act, and think about your impact on your own life. In many ways I think of this book is not a book about self-hypnosis; rather, a book about self-improvement and self-betterment. I know these inductions work, because I use them myself.

To help you set some goals for yourself I have included at the back of this book some smart goal setting templates, as well as three questions you should ask yourself when coming up with goals for yourself. These three questions have been proven by psychologists to drastically improve the chances that your goals will be completed successfully if you can emphatically answer yes to each of these three questions whenever coming up with a new goal for yourself. This is my gift to you, for purchasing this book and having faith in me and more importantly suspending your belief and disbelief so that you can hypnotize yourself easily, effortlessly, and without any of the challenges that many people argue they have.

On this note, I will bid you farewell, and invite you to visit my company's website: www.indirect knowledge.com. Here, you will find other hypnosis and neurolinguistic programming resources that can also aid you in improving your life and helping other people to improve there's.

Again thank you for purchasing this book!

Learn well! Live well!

Bryan Westra

INDEX

ABOUT THE AUTHOR

Bryan Westra is a prominent lecturer and trainer. His background is in Hypnosis and NLP. He holds advanced degrees in Organizational Behavior, Sales, Marketing, Management, and Counseling. He is also the founder of Indirect Knowledge Limited.

www.indirectknowledge.com

OTHER BOOKS BY THE AUTHOR

Hypnotic Storytelling by Bryan Westra
Link: http://amzn.com/B00KMWR7DO

Indirect Knowledge by Bryan Westra
Link: http://amzn.com/B009EAWSTI

NLP & Hypnosis Influence and Persuasion Patterns by Bryan James Westra
Link: http://amzn.com/B00F1I8WC4

A Manual for Creating Conversational Hypnotists: The Answers You Want by Bryan James Westra
Link: http://amzn.com/0989946487

Learn & Remember 25 Secret Hypnotic Language Patterns Now to Help You Become Rich: Change Minds, Earn More, Win by Bryan Westra
Link: http://amzn.com/0990513211

Secret Sales Hypnosis: Work Less, Be Number 1, Explode Your Bank Account by Bryan Westra
Link: http://amzn.com/0615782191

S.M.A.R.T. GOALS

SPECIFIC

MEASURABLE

ACTIONABLE

REALISTIC

TIMELY

S.M.A.R.T. GOALS

SPECIFIC

MEASURABLE

ACTIONABLE

REALISTIC

TIMELY

S.M.A.R.T. GOALS

SPECIFIC

MEASURABLE

ACTIONABLE

REALISTIC

TIMELY

S.M.A.R.T. GOALS

SPECIFIC

MEASURABLE

ACTIONABLE

REALISTIC

TIMELY

S.M.A.R.T. GOALS

SPECIFIC

MEASURABLE

ACTIONABLE

REALISTIC

TIMELY

CAN IT BE DONE?

WILL IT WORK?

IS IT WORTH IT?